Statistics
& Measurement

Statistics
& Measurement

AN INTRODUCTION

4TH EDITION

RAY M. ZEISSET

Center for Applications of Psychological Type, Inc. · 2815 NW 13th St., Suite 401 · Gainesville, FL 32609 · www.capt.org

Published by
Center for Applications of Psychological Type, Inc.
2815 NW 13th Street, Suite 401
Gainesville FL 32609
352.375.0160
www.capt.org

Center for Applications of Psychological Type, Inc. and CAPT are trademarks or registered trademarks of the Center for Applications of Psychological Type in the United States and other countries.

Myers-Briggs Type Indicator, Myers-Briggs, and MBTI are trademarks or registered trademarks of the MBTI Trust, Inc. in the United States and other countries.

Murphy-Meisgeier Type Indicator for Children and MMTIC are trademarks of Elizabeth Murphy and Charles Meisgeier in the United States and other countries.

Library of Congress Cataloging-in-Publication Data

Zeisset, Ray M., 1939-
    Statistics & measurement : an introduction / Ray M. Zeisset. -- 4th ed.
        p. cm.
    Rev. ed. of: Statistics and measurement. 3rd ed. c2000.
    Includes bibliographical references and index.
    ISBN 978-0-935652-90-1 (pbk.)
1. Psychometrics. 2. Psychological tests. 3. Myers-Briggs Type
Indicator. I. Zeisset, Ray M., 1939- Statistics and measurement. II.
Title. III. Title: Statistics and measurement.

    BF39.Z45 2009
    150.1'5195--dc22

2009037916

To Carolyn

TABLE OF CONTENTS

PART 1
Basic Statistics

Chapter 3 *Inferential Statistics*

PART 3
Reading Research Critically

APPENDICES

Foreword

IN HIS PREFACE and chapter 1, author Ray Zeisset has done such a thorough job of introducing this book that a foreword in the usual sense isn't needed. But a little history might be useful. Ray was one of the earliest trainers helping to prepare people to use the Myers-Briggs Type Indicator® instrument. His knowledge of statistics and psychological instrument development was invaluable to the other trainers, and we urged him to write training components that we who had never taught statistics could use. We were delighted when this book was first published.

As we all gained experience in using his book and gathered feedback about it from training participants, we thought we saw ways that it could be made more user-friendly and effective. Ray was warmly receptive to our suggestions. So the second edition came into being incorporating the ideas of trainers and participants.

In every training session we had some participants who had never experienced statistics before, many of them fearful of this part of the training. They were amazed at how well Ray's book made the work flow for them. Every training group also included participants who had taken statistics or tests and measurement courses in college. Uniformly they praised Ray's book and most of them reported it to be more clear and helpful than the college texts they had used.

The second edition got massaged in a similar way by the experiences of trainers and participants and the third edition was born. Now we have a *new* edition that, for the first time, has quizlike exercises at the end of the chapters in parts I and II that are typical of those used in the MBTI® certification training. Other helpful features have been added. The chapter overview summaries, the learning keys throughout each chapter, and the exercises at the end of each section are the essence of the condensation that is the nature of this book, and they all provide an excellent way to review what has been covered. The new part III is Ray's way of showing us we can all be better consumers of research reports by learning how to read intelligently the research design and data tables we encounter.

As trainers we have said repeatedly—and training participants have echoed the sentiment—that we wish we'd had this book in graduate school when we were taking statistics and measurement courses. If you've had those courses before, we believe you will be pleasantly surprised at how well this book distills and clarifies many of the things you have already studied. For those of you new to statistics or measurement, we believe you are getting an outstanding introduction that is understandable, relevant, and useful. This book provides a matchless beginning for learning to be a knowledgeable consumer of information for any subject, and particularly on psychological assessment tools. This work will help you become a confident, credible, and ethical user of the MBTI instrument.

Statistics and Measurement is obviously a labor of love by an author who cares a lot about connecting with readers and helping them become at ease with concepts and techniques that they might have considered to be daunting. After finishing the book, we hope and believe that many of you will find yourself saying "It really wasn't so hard" and "Now I truly understand some things about statistics and measurement that I never really grasped before."

Best wishes for a superior learning experience from this committed, caring and exceptionally knowledgeable teacher and the work he presents.

Gordon Lawrence and Charles Martin

Preface

IT'S A COMMON experience. At the beginning of a training session in the use of a psychological instrument, or at the start of a college class, I hear statements such as these from participants.

"I'm really interested in learning to use this instrument, but I'm nervous about having to learn about the statistics."

"I haven't had statistics before. I've never been very good with math. I hope this won't be too hard."

"I had a statistics course once, but it was a long time ago, and I didn't understand it then, and I don't remember it now."

Through the pages of this book, I hope to introduce some basic concepts of statistics and measurement to people who want to use or understand psychological tests and research instruments but do not have a background in math or statistics. The intention is to help the reader understand research literature and test manuals without feeling intimidated by the statistical concepts. Overview summaries at the beginning of each section, make this book a useful refresher on key concepts long after its initial use.

Statistics & Measurement is not intended to make you a statistician or prepare you to do research. For that you'll either need extensive university-level training, or you'll need to team up with someone who has such training. However, this study can help you understand the basic statistical and measurement concepts presented in research and test manuals. It can help you weigh the evidence for and against techniques and approaches that interest you, and it can also help you use psychological assessment tools more effectively.

The development of this book began over two decades ago, when my wife and I began offering certification training for users of the Myers-Briggs Type Indicator® instrument. At the time, providers of such training were using three different books to introduce the statistics and measurement concepts needed to use the MBTI® instrument well, but none of those books were intended for people without prior knowledge of statistics, and none dealt with the variety of issues specific to a personality type instrument. This book has been developed to provide a single source for general *and* MBTI-specific statistics and measurement principles at a level that does not require prior study of statistics. After several unpublished versions, *Statistics & Measurement: An Introduction for MBTI Users* was published by the Center for Applications of Psychological Type in 1994, and revised editions appeared in 1996 and 2000.

Through the years, many of our certification participants with prior statistics backgrounds have commented that by using this book they came to understand statistics and measurement in ways they never had before. Recognizing that this work could meet the needs of a wider group than our original audience, each successive edition has expanded the coverage to more general topics. After many years as a practicing clinical psychologist, I began teaching basic research and assessment courses in a graduate program for professional counselors. I have used previous editions of this book in those classes, and my students and their questions have contributed to the development of this edition.

The book does use many examples from the MBTI instrument, both because it is widely known and because it illustrates statistical and measurement concepts that are basic to many psychological tests. This assessment also illustrates some of the latest in test construction technology. Appendix A provides a brief introduction to psychological type for those unfamiliar with the MBTI instrument.

We know from our understanding of personality type, as well as from a large body of educational research on learning styles, that we don't all learn in the same way. Some parts of this material likely will really fit for you, and other parts will not seem as helpful. There may be more details and examples than some types care for or need, but other types of learners may find those same parts the key to more complete understanding. I have tried to meet the needs of a broad range of learning styles through approaching topics in a variety of ways.

While I teach basic statistics to my students, I am not a statistician. Instead, I am a clinical psychologist who has learned over the years how many people have strong fears and mental blocks when it comes to numbers. I'll try to lead you through this material as gently as I can. To help make this material as easy as possible, I have tried to avoid terms and concepts that you are not likely to need as a research reader or test user, and I've used a few simple examples repeatedly so you can see how different concepts relate to each other.

New for this edition. In this edition of *Statistics & Measurement*, each section begins with an overview to orient the reader to the content or to refresh one's memory. More examples from a variety of areas have been added, and there are expanded exercises and questions for you to check your understanding at the end of each chapter. Many topics have been extensively updated. Part III is a new section with a guide to critically reading research.

How This Book Is Organized

Part I deals with basic statistics and includes an introduction to descriptive statistics (chapter 2), that is, statistics used to describe or summarize data that have been collected. While describing data efficiently is helpful, much of our scientific interest is in generalizing from data to the broader world. Inferential statistics (chapter 3) allow us to determine whether the differences noted in data are large enough to call them significant, that is, to comfortably assume they probably did not happen just by chance, so that our findings can be generalized beyond the sample group.

Part II deals with characteristics of good psychological tests, emphasizing reliability (chapter 4) and validity (chapter 5). Chapter 6 deals with norms—data that provide us a way of interpreting scores—and usability—qualities that make a test user-friendly.

Part III aims to help you apply your new knowledge. Lack of understanding— and fear—of the statistics involved is a reason many people give for avoiding the reading of journal articles. Part III, "Reading Research Critically," focuses on how to use the understanding gained in parts I and II to read whole research articles, not just abstracts.

Also scattered throughout the text are learning key boxes that highlight definitions of key concepts. You can use these definitions to focus your reading of the text as well as to check your understanding. Terms that appear in boldface have learning key definitions. Each chapter concludes with several exercises or questions so you can check your understanding of the material you have read.

The book concludes with several appendixes. Appendix A provides an introduction to personality type. Appendix B extends the discussion from chapter 3 on tests of significance and illustrates several applications of significance tests. Appendix C presents a special use of Chi-square for personality type research. Appendix D expands the discussion from chapter 3 of one- and two-tailed tests of significance. Appendix E provides answers to the exercises and questions at the ends of chapters.

This preface began with common statements from people as they enter a training session or college course where they will learn or review some basic things about statistics and measurement. The good news is that many of these same people leave the training with comments such as these:

"That wasn't so hard."

"I actually enjoyed the simple, step-by-step way the statistics part of the training was presented."

"Now I understand some things about statistics that I've heard about but never understood before."

My hope is that after you work your way through this book, you too can make a comment such as these.

Ray Zeisset, Lincoln, Nebraska

Acknowledgements

I AM DEEPLY grateful to the many people who have contributed to the development of this book. I am especially indebted to Gordon Lawrence and the late Mary McCaulley, who recognized the importance and encouraged the vision for this work and made helpful suggestions along the way. Gerald Macdaid, Margaret Fields, and Charles Martin were helpful in the development of the first three editions, and Judy Breiner, Jamelyn R. Johnson, and Eleanor Sommer have supported the work of this edition.

Participants in Prairie View and Zeisset Associates certification workshops were the impetus for this work and have aided in the refinement process over the years. My students in the Master of Arts in Counseling program at Doane College have provided me with a forum to hone my passion for making statistics and measurement understandable, and several have made some important suggestions. Jean Piccini assisted with graphics. My statistician daughter, Michelle Zeisset, and my statistician brother, Paul Zeisset, have contributed significantly as well.

My greatest debt, however, is to my wife and partner, Carolyn, who has been an integral part of the development of this work over the past two decades. In early versions, every sentence had to be rewritten until she was satisfied that it was understandable to her and others without any prior statistical or measurement background. As an INFP, she is well aware that my ISFJ way of saying things is not always easy for other types to understand, and she has made innumerable suggestions for better ways to say things. For this edition, her command of the content in suggesting major substantive improvements has been impressive. To her this edition is gratefully dedicated.

The references and selected bibliography include many sources that have provided helpful information that is woven into these pages. I want to particularly acknowledge the contributions of the Kimble; Morgan and King; and Munro, Visintainer, and Page texts for illustrating understandable ways to present statistics; to the Kaplan and Saccuzzo and the Erford texts for their coverage of recent developments in psychometrics; and to the Meltzoff, Nieswiadomy, and Stanovich texts for their background on the process of critically reading research.

1

Basic Statistics

Because the study of statistics and measurement is one that many people avoid, we begin part I with the often-heard question, "Why bother?" What makes this study worthwhile? Chapter 1 offers a variety of answers.

Statistics are used for two basic purposes:

- to describe or summarize a group of numbers—some data, and

- to help us know how likely it is that the differences we find in data could have happened by chance alone.

We consider the first purpose, summarizing data, in chapter 2 on descriptive statistics. The second purpose, determining how likely a finding happened by chance, is addressed in chapter 3 on inferential statistics.

1
Why Bother?

Questions frequently asked by people I teach are "Why do we have to learn statistics, anyway? Why bother? Why not just ask other people what they use, and be done with it?"

Understanding statistics can help us in a variety of ways. As professionals, understanding statistics and measurement can help us understand and use the available literature in test manuals and research articles. As consumers, understanding statistical principles can help us avoid being misled by some of the deceptive ways statistics can be used.

Understanding statistics and measurement helps us have confidence in the instruments and procedures we use. When we understand the basis for what we are using, we are able to defend our choice of procedures if questioned or challenged. When we are familiar with the vocabulary of statistics, we can converse with a degree of credibility with others who use the same assessment tools, as well as with skeptical professionals and potential clients.

When we understand statistics and measurement ourselves, we are better able to hear and respond to the questions that clients may have regarding measurement issues related to the instruments being used. I frequently get comments from participants in training suggesting that clients never ask such questions. I just smile when I hear from them a short time after the training that, lo and behold, a client asked a question about the reliability or validity of the instrument. These practitioners now can hear the practical questions people have about measurement principles. Not only can we answer the simple questions, but when confronted with more complex questions from more knowledgeable clients, we can point to the appropriate data in a test manual or a journal.

Periodically articles appear in the popular press that question the usefulness of one psychological instrument or another. Often such stories contain errors about the intended use of the instruments, their construction, and the research on reliability and validity. Practitioners who do not understand construction, reliability, and validity issues may accept the assumptions of an article's authors and move away from using an effective instrument. However, practitioners who have a basic understanding of these issues can question the assumptions and review the evidence, pro and con. At the very least they can point themselves and others to sources that answer the questions and make an informed decision about whether or not to move forward in their use of the instrument.

Readers who are used to living in a world of trade secrets and proprietary information may be unaware that one of the hallmarks of psychology as a science is publicly verifiable knowledge. Trade secrets are not recognized in the area of psychological assessments and procedures. An instrument can be copyrighted after it is developed, of course, so that unauthorized duplication does not occur, but information about its development and research, which verifies its effectiveness, must be accessible to professionals and the interested public. Publicly verifiable knowledge means that research done in relation to an instrument has been published in peer-reviewed journals. Peer review means that an article has been critically reviewed by professionals experienced in the subject matter and meets specific standards in order to be accepted for publication in a journal. The author is expected to fully disclose information about the research so others can evaluate it or replicate it—that is, do the experiment again with a different group of people to see if the findings hold.

We thus can expect that information is available about tests and procedures that we may want to use. That information can help us determine if the tests or procedures are appropriate for our needs. In addition, we will want to know the way scientific findings are reported and how to interpret the statistical information provided.

What are Statistics?

Statistics are numbers with a story to tell. So said the sign I saw in a science museum exhibit several years ago. So what's the story? As we will see, statistics are numbers that serve two basic purposes. They describe or summarize information, and they help us know if the numbers—the data we find in an experiment—are more than could be explained by chance alone.

4

In describing data, we want to find the middle of our numbers. That is, what is the *average*? We want to know how spread out the numbers are. Are the numbers clustered closely together, or are they spread far apart? We may want to know if there is a relationship between one set of numbers and another set of numbers. We wonder if the numbers are *correlated*.

In looking to see if we have more than chance, we become aware of the probabilistic nature of science. Nothing is certain. We are asking, *what are the odds* that this is a chance finding? The answers to these questions are always answered in probabilities. *There are no absolute certainties in statistics.*

As we apply statistics to tests and procedures, we want to know how *consistently* the tests and procedures measure what they measure. We also want to know whether our instruments really are measuring what they are intended to measure.

Through it all, we will want the statistics and measurement that support the instruments we are interested in to be presented with clarity and fairness. Statistics are not just cut-and-dried sets of facts. Instead, *statistics are sets of facts put together with a variety of assumptions and possible interpretations.* We want those who present us with this information to use both good judgment and common sense, so that we can learn the story accurately. When we have occasion to present data to others, we will want to do it with good judgment and common sense as well.

I hope this book helps you find, and understand, the story in the numbers you encounter.

Why are Statistics Important?

Even though we have some idea about what statistics are, we may still ask, why bother wading through all that information? Why not just get some testimonials from other people who have used procedures we might be interested in? One of the principles of psychology as a science is that case studies and testimonials have limited value. They do not provide what science considers proof. The usefulness of case studies is in the earliest stages of an investigation, when we are trying to find interesting phenomena and variables to study. In later stages of study, case studies are generally of little value for two reasons: —the *placebo* effect and the *vividness* effect.

The placebo effect is the tendency for people to report that *any* treatment has helped. People tend to believe they have been given something to help them, and indeed the hopeful attitude that results from the belief that something is being done is often associated with improvement. However, the placebo effect makes it possible to get testimonials to support the effectiveness of any procedure, regardless of the value of the procedure.

The vividness effect leads people to weight testimonial evidence heavily in considering alternatives. Testimonial information is more vivid and thus more retrievable from memory than other information. For example, I may study a consumer magazine to determine which piece of new technology I want to buy. Armed with the magazine's recommendations, I proceed to the technology store to buy the new piece of equipment. Once in the store, while I am looking for the recommended product, a salesperson approaches me and offers to help. The salesperson suggests that another product is the one he uses, and he tells me how happy he has been with it and how well it works. I am likely to walk out of the store with the product he recommends, because his recommendation is more *vivid* than the gray statistics in the magazine.

Understanding the fact that testimonials do not provide evidence helps us understand why it is so important to gather statistical information about instruments and procedures we might want to use in professional practice. Such knowledge may also help us be better consumers in our personal lives by helping us to avoid overvaluing testimonial information as we consider the purchase of products and services.

The purpose of this book is to give you some language and tools to help you evaluate statistical information as you use psychological instruments and procedures in your profession. There is usually plenty of objective information about various tests and procedures available in databases and journals. The challenge is to be able to decipher and understand that information. The aim of this book is to help you feel sufficiently comfortable with basic statistical knowledge so that you can dig into that objective information as you seek to make informed decisions.

So just relax, get comfortable, and start working your way through this material. You will understand some parts quickly, while you will need to go over other parts several times. But be assured, you *can* learn these concepts and they *will be* helpful to you, sooner than you think.

2
Descriptive Statistics

The first basic purpose of statistics is to describe or summarize groups of numbers, typically called *data*. A large group of numbers in no particular order is unlikely to be very helpful, but if we organize the numbers and summarize them, we may provide useful information. Our survey of descriptive statistics will include frequency distributions, measures of central tendency, measures of variability, and correlation.

Frequency Distributions

At the simplest level, data can be summarized by counting the number of individuals who got each possible score and showing this in a table or in a graph.

Overview

A **frequency distribution** is a display, either in table or graph form, of groups or intervals of numbers (scores from tests or data from measurements) and the frequency—or number of occurrences—in each. While the precise value of each individual score may be lost, information is summarized so that we can quickly see what the data show.

When displayed in a graph, frequency is represented by the height of the bar or the line above the baseline. Scores on the **variable** being measured are represented on the baseline, from the lowest score at the left to the highest score at the far right. The higher the bar or the line of the curve is above the baseline, the higher the frequency at that point on the scale.

In the frequency distributions of many psychological characteristics, most scores fall in the middle of the distribution, with fewer and fewer scores found toward the low and high extremes. These distributions also tend to be symmetrical. Many frequency polygons approach a shape known as the bell-shaped **normal curve**. If scores tend to pile up at one end or the other of the distribution, it is called a *skewed distribution.*

Let's suppose we are in the business of manufacturing products for children, and we are interested in physical characteristics of eight-year-olds. We gather the heights of 50 of these children and find the data in table 2.1.

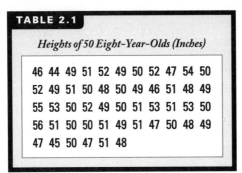

TABLE 2.1

Heights of 50 Eight-Year-Olds (Inches)

46	44	49	51	52	49	50	52	47	54	50
52	49	51	50	48	50	49	46	51	48	49
55	53	50	52	49	50	51	53	51	53	50
56	51	50	50	51	49	51	47	50	48	49
47	45	50	47	51	48					

This information does not make a lot of sense simply as a listing of 50 different numbers. We need to organize and summarize them so that the information is meaningful. One way to do this is to set up intervals, as we have done in table 2.2, and tally how many numbers fall in each interval. After tallying our observations, we put the number of observations in each interval under the heading f, where f = frequency.

We can also display summarized tabulation of heights in a graph, as shown in figure 2.1. If you rotate the page 90 degrees counter-clockwise, you'll see the same shape in the tally marks as we have in the graph.

A **frequency distribution** is a display, either in table form or graph form, of measurement groups or intervals and the frequency (number of occurrences) in each. Both table 2.2 (omitting the tally marks) and figure 2.1 are frequency distributions. A frequency distribution loses the identity of each individual measurement and may even lose the precise value of any individual measurement. However, we gain more than we lose because we now have our information organized so that we can quickly get an impression of what it shows.

You will note in figure 2.1 that the vertical axis of the frequency polygon (what a graphical frequency distribution is

TABLE 2.2

Tabulation of Heights

Inches	Tally	f
43–44	I	1
45–46	III	3
47–48	⊬⊬ III	8
49–50	⊬⊬ ⊬⊬ ⊬⊬ IIII	19
51–52	⊬⊬ ⊬⊬ III	13
53–54	IIII	4
55–56	II	2

sometimes called) represents the number of cases observed and goes from 1, or the lowest number observed, at the baseline to the highest number at the top. The horizontal axis represents the scores of individuals on the variable being measured, going from 1 or the lowest number observed at the left corner to the highest score observed at the far right. This is the typical way to display distributions. In distributions the higher the curve is above the baseline, the higher the frequency at that point

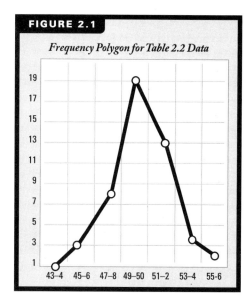

FIGURE 2.1

Frequency Polygon for Table 2.2 Data

on the scale along the baseline. *Low scores are always on the left and high scores on the right.*

In the foregoing discussion, we used the word **variable**. What is a variable? A variable is any characteristic of an object, event, person, or whatever, that can take on two or more *values*. Eye color and age are variables because there is more than one value each can take (brown eyes, blue eyes, green eyes; age 1, age 17, age 92, and so forth). You and I are not variables because there is only one of each of us. We'll be seeing the word *variable* often.

It is important that we have ways, such as frequency distributions, to organize data with lots of numbers because, for most purposes, one lone measurement is of little value. A single reading of a thermometer would do us little good if we want to know how warmly to dress. We need to consider past experience–that is, generalizations from lots of other readings—to have a frame of reference for knowing whether a particular temperature will seem warm or chilly. In building chairs or producing clothes for eight-year-olds, we can't measure just one child and hope that works as a basis for making our product. We need measurements from many children.

Learning Key

Frequency distributions: Display of data in table or graph form, dividing the range of scores into intervals and counting the number of occurrences (frequency) in each interval.

Variable: A characteristic that can take on two or more values (eyes are brown or blue or green).

The distribution of scores in many frequency distributions of psychological characteristics is such that most of the scores fall in the middle of the distribution, while fewer and fewer scores are found toward the low and high extremes of the distribution. Most distributions also tend to be symmetrical; about as many scores are found at the low end, called the *negative end*, as at the high, or *positive, end*. In general, the more measurements we take, the smoother the graph becomes, because many of the irregularities are the result of chance variations in the population measured. Both mathematically and experimentally it has been shown that many frequency polygons eventually approach a shape known as the normal curve, the outline of which is shown in figure 2.2.

If for some reason larger numbers of individuals score at one end or the other of the distribution, the distribution is not symmetrical and it is called a *skewed distribution*. In figure 2.2, you will note that *skewed distributions* can be either negatively skewed or positively skewed. In a negatively skewed distribution, the tail of the distribution points to the negative end of the scale. In a positive skew, scores are bunched up in the low end of the distribution and the tail points to the positive or high end of the scale.

While many characteristics are normally distributed, not all frequency distributions have the shape of a normal curve, or even a skewed bell-shaped curve. Personality type as measured by an assessment like the Myers-Briggs Type Indicator® (MBTI®) instrument does not have a normal distribution. Instead, the frequency of each of the 16 types is presented in a special type table format, which is itself a type of frequency distribution, an example of which is shown in figure 2.3. The U.S. Census data shows other irregular distributions, for example the number of children per household (where 0 is the most frequent value), or the number of paid employees per business (about three-fourths of all businesses have no paid employees; the person is self-employed). This distribution is shown in figure 2.4. Examining a frequency distribution helps us see how normal our results are.

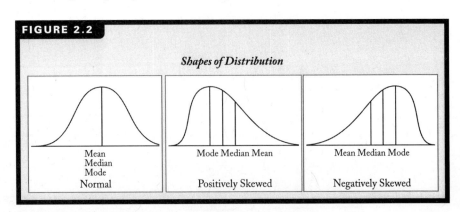

FIGURE 2.2

Shapes of Distribution

Mean Median Mode	Mode Median Mean	Mean Median Mode
Normal	Positively Skewed	Negatively Skewed

FIGURE 2.3

Estimated Frequencies of the Types in the United States Population

ISTJ	ISFJ	INFJ	INTJ
11–14%	9–14%	1–3%	2–4%
11.6%	13.8%	1.5%	2.1%

ISTP	ISFP	INFP	INTP
4–6%	5–9%	4–5%	3–5%
5.4%	8.8%	4.4%	3.3%

ESTP	ESFP	ENFP	ENTP
4–5%	4–9%	6–8%	2–5%
4.3%	8.5%	8.1%	3.2%

ESTJ	ESFJ	ENFJ	ENTJ
8–12%	9–13%	2–5%	2–5%
8.7%	12.3%	2.5%	1.8%

■ = approximately one percent

Given the disparity in type frequencies found in different studies, ranges of percentages are presented to capture the most probable area in which the true frequency of a type falls.

E	45–53%	49.3%	S	66–74%	73.3%	T	40–50%	40.2%	J	54–60%	54.1%
I	47–55%	50.7%	N	26–34%	26.7%	F	50–60%	59.8%	P	40–46%	45.9%

From *Looking at Type: The Fundamentals* by Charles Martin (CAPT 1997). Used with permission.

FIGURE 2.4

Firms by Number of Employees, 2004

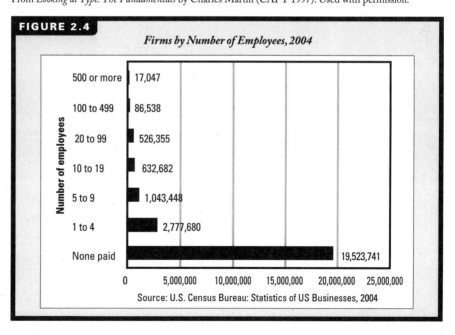

Source: U.S. Census Bureau: Statistics of US Businesses, 2004

Organizing a set of numbers into a frequency distribution allows us to look over our data and get a general sense of what the numbers show. However, we often need more detailed analysis. For this, we have three general kinds of measures: measures of central tendency, or averages; measures of variability, how much spread there is among the scores; and correlation coefficients, which measure the relationship between two variables.

Before we can look at these measures more specifically, we need to introduce the concept of levels of measurement. There are a variety of measures of central tendency, measures of variability, and correlation coefficients, and the choice of which one to use in any situation is based in part on the level of measurement of the data. We will also consider the distinction between discrete and continuous data.

Kinds of Measurement

Measurement is the assignment of numbers to objects or events according to rules. Three sets of rules are commonly used in the behavioral sciences: nominal measurement, ordinal measurement, and interval measurement. Understanding these distinctions is important because they effect which measures of central tendency, variability, and correlation are appropriate to use in a given situation.

Overview

Nominal measurement involves *classifying* or *sorting* things into mutually exclusive categories so that everything in each category is alike in some respect, such as apples and oranges; male and female, or animal, vegetable, and mineral.

Ordinal measurement involves *ranking* things. When we rank, we know that the highest rank is greater than the second, and the second is higher than the third, as with military ranks and movie ratings, but we are not measuring how large the interval is between each.

Interval measurement measures the *magnitude of the difference* between one thing and another. Equal differences along the scale represent equal differences in what is measured, for example, age or height. **Ratio measurement** is a special kind of interval measurement applicable when there is a true zero. In the behavioral sciences we rarely have true zeroes, so we only need to be concerned with nominal, ordinal, or interval measurement.

Another distinction often made in statistics is between discrete and continuous data. **Discrete data** are whole numbers and usually come from counts or frequencies, as in the number of persons per household. With **continuous data**, observations are not limited to whole numbers but can take on an unlimited number of intermediate values, such as age or height. Most psychological test data are discrete data. Scores on most tests are the result of counts of whole numbers, the number of items answered in a particular way. However, scores are often converted to, or treated as, **continuous scores** in research, as is done in many of the reliability studies reported in test manuals. Scores are treated *as if* they are continuous data.

When we measure, we are assigning numbers to objects or events according to some rules that transform qualities of things into numbers. If some wine-tasters want to rate wines, they can establish a rule that a very bad wine is a 1 and a very outstanding wine is a 10. For wine judging to work, the set of rules must be clearly defined, and this set of rules becomes a scale of measurement. Many sets of rules are possible, but in the behavioral sciences we typically use just three sets of rules that define nominal measurement, ordinal measurement, and interval measurement.

Scales of measurement differ from each other based on three characteristics: magnitude, equal intervals, and an absolute zero. Magnitude means some instances have more, less, or equal amounts of what we are looking at than other instances do. For equal intervals, we ask if the difference between two points at one place on the scale has the same meaning as the difference between two other points on the scale with the same number of units of difference. An absolute zero measurement means that nothing of the property we are interested in exists. We will see these distinctions play out as we look at these levels of measurement.

Levels of Measurement

Nominal measurement involves *classifying* or *sorting* things into mutually exclusive categories so that all the things in one category are alike in some respect. Nominal scales aren't really scales at all; their purpose is to serve as identification tags for different categories of things. For example, if we took a basket of mixed fruit and sorted it into separate piles of bananas, oranges, and apples, we would be involved in nominal measurement. We could assign bananas as 1, oranges as 2, and apples as 3, or apples could be 1, bananas 2 and oranges 3; it doesn't matter. The numbers only function is to help us group all the instances of each category. Counting the number of Extraverts (Es) and Introverts (Is) in a group, or the number within each of the 16 MBTI types on a type table, gives us nominal data. The numbers on the back of basketball jerseys, and Social Security, license plate, and telephone numbers are all nominal measurement. In terms of the three characteristics of measurement scales, nominal measurement does not have magnitude, equal intervals, or an absolute zero. Something either fits in a category or it doesn't.

Ordinal measurement involves *ranking* things according to some attribute. If you rank order your preferences for fruit and give oranges a rank of 1 or first, apples a 2 (second), and bananas a 3 (third), you would be making an ordinal measurement. We know you like oranges better than apples, and apples better than bananas, but we have no idea how large the interval is between your first and second choice, or how it compares with the interval between your second and third choice. All we know is that the first rank is higher than the second, and the second is higher than the third. If we had a class arrange themselves in a line from tallest to shortest, we would have ordinal measurement. We would know Student B is taller than Student C, and we would know Student C is taller than Student D, but we would not be measuring how much taller B is than C, or how that interval compares to the difference between C and D. In ordinal measurement, we have magnitude, but do not have equal intervals or absolute zero. We know three-star movies are supposed to be better than two-star, but we do not know how much better they are.

In **interval measurement** we measure the *magnitude of the difference* between one thing and another. For example, when we compare temperatures on a thermometer, equal differences along the scale represent equal differences in temperature change. As in a lot of interval measurement, we don't have a true zero in our temperature readings. For example, the Fahrenheit (F) and Celsius (C) scales have

Learning Key

Nominal measurement: Sorting into mutually exclusive categories (apples vs. oranges).

Ordinal measurement: Ranking things (1st, 2nd, 3rd; oranges better than apples, and apples better than bananas).

Interval measurement: Magnitude of difference between one thing and another can be measured because intervals along scale are equal (42°F-32° same as 52°-42°).

Ratio measurement: Interval measurement in which there are true zeroes; 0 = nothing (5 inches, 10 pounds).

Discrete data: Only whole numbers (1, 17, 92); usually counts (frequencies).

Continuous data: Measurement with unlimited intermediate values between whole numbers, like 3.773429; not limited to whole numbers. For research purposes, scores on a test may be treated *as if* they are on a continuous scale.

different zero points and neither is at the bottom of the possible temperature scale, but at least our temperature numbers do represent meaningful differences in magnitude. A 20 degree difference between 30 degrees and 50 degrees is comparable to the difference between 40 degrees and 60 degrees. With interval measurement, then, we have both magnitude and equal intervals.

When researchers look for correlations between scales on a test and other measures, they treat the scores *as if* they were interval data. They assume that the difference between scores of 7 and 17 is the same as between 11 and 21. Interval data, being on a scale with consistent intervals, can be added while ordinal data cannot. We can't add ranks. In actuality, scores on many psychological instruments are closer to being ordinal measurement than interval but, for research purposes, scores are treated as interval data.

Ratio measurement is a special kind of interval measurement. When we are measuring something with a true zero, as we would be if we were using a ruler or yardstick, our measurement is on a ratio scale. It not only has equal intervals, but also begins at an *absolute zero* so that ratios can be calculated. We can say that 10 inches is twice as long as 5 inches, because zero inches is a real zero. Zero equals nothing in this case. Making ratio comparisons is something we can't do without an absolute or true zero. With interval measurement, we can make ratio comparisons of the size of intervals, or differences, but not of the scores themselves. For example, we can say that a rise of 20 degrees F is half as great as a 40-degree rise, because in interval measurement we can trust the magnitude of differences. However, we cannot say a balmy 80-degree day is twice as warm as a cool 40-degree day, because the Fahrenheit scale is not a ratio scale with a true zero. A ratio measurement has magnitude, equal intervals, and an absolute zero.

You needn't worry much about ratio measurement, except to know that in the behavioral sciences we rarely have true zeroes. Your primary concern will be with nominal, ordinal, and interval measurement.

FIGURE 2.5

Levels of Measurement

Nominal (Sorting)		Ordinal (Ranking)	Interval (Measuring Magnitude)	Ratio (True Zeroes)
Oranges	Apples	1st	_____ 40° F	4 inches
E	I	2nd	_____ 30° F	3 inches
J	P	3rd	_____ 20° F	2 inches
Male	Female	4th	_____ 10° F	1 inch
Group A	Group B			0 inches

When we work with data, it is important to be aware of what kind of measurement we have because the choice of statistical techniques to use depends on whether we have nominal, ordinal or interval data. Figure 2.5 illustrates the levels of measurement.

Discrete and Continuous Data

Another distinction frequently made in measurement is between discrete and continuous data. **Discrete data** are usually counts or frequencies. When we count the number of men in our class, we have a discrete number, a whole number. We will not have 3.795 men! When we have **continuous data**, our observations are not limited to whole numbers but can take on an unlimited number of intermediate values. For example, when we take temperature measurements, an unlimited number of values are possible. We may say it is 73 degrees when it may really be 72.687 degrees. We say 73 for convenience or because of the limitations of our thermometer or our eyesight.

With most psychological test data we are generally talking about discrete data. Scores on most tests are the result of counts of whole numbers, counting the number of items answered in a particular way. However, scores are often converted to, or treated as, **continuous scores** in research, as is done in many of the reliability studies reported in test manuals. Scores are treated *as if* they are continuous data. Don't worry; statisticians have ways of determining when things can be treated *as if* they are something else without great harm. At this point, we can trust their judgment that it is OK. Just be aware that when you see reliability studies for a test using continuous scores, the scores are being treated as if the possible scores are not limited to whole numbers.

Now that we have discussed frequency distributions and kinds of measurement, we are ready to look at three general kinds of measures that are used with data when we need a more detailed analysis than what we can do with a frequency distribution. The methods used for these more detailed analyses are measures of central tendency, measures of variability, and correlation coefficients. We look first at measures of central tendency.

Measures of Central Tendency

Measures of central tendency are numbers that fix the *center* of a distribution. Defining the center depends in part on what kind of measurements we have.

Overview

Measures of central tendency are numbers that define the *center* of a distribution. Three measures of central tendency are commonly used in the behavioral sciences: the mean, the median, and the mode. Which one we use depends in part on what kind of measurements we have.

The most familiar is the arithmetic **mean**, which can be used when we have interval measurement. The commonly used symbol for the mean is $\overline{X}$. To obtain the mean, we add up all the scores and divide by the total number (N or n) of observations.

The **median** is the middle score in a group of ranked measurements, and is the point at which 50% of the measurements are below, and 50% are above that point. The median is appropriately used with ordinal measurement, but it can also be used for interval measurement. The median is generally the preferred measure for skewed distributions, even when we have interval measurement, because it is not influenced so much by extreme scores.

The **mode** is the most frequent score. The mode is the *only* measure that can be used with nominal measurements. There may be more than one mode in a distribution.

In a theoretically perfect frequency distribution known as the **normal curve**, the mean, median, and mode are all the same, and the shape is a symmetrical bell-shaped curve.

Mean

The most familiar of the measures of central tendency is the arithmetic **mean,** what most people think of when you say the word average. The mean can be used when we have interval measurement. The commonly used symbol for the mean is $\overline{X}$, pronounced *X-bar*. To obtain the mean, we add up all the measurements and divide by the total number (N or n) in the group.

The mean can be used meaningfully only with interval measurement because it gives every measurement in the distribution equal weight, which implies that all magnitudes of differences between measurements are to be trusted.

Median

The **median** is the middle score in a group of measurements that have been rank-ordered from lowest to highest, or highest to lowest. In this case 50% of the measurements will fall below the median, and 50% will fall above. An easy way to remember the median is to think of the median of a freeway: half of the roadway is to the left and half is to the right. The median is the appropriate measure of central tendency for ordinal measurements because the middle score is the middle rank. We also can use the median for interval measurement.

The median is generally the preferred measure for skewed distributions, even when we have interval measurement. The median is not influenced so much by extreme scores. When people asked me about the length of stay of patients in the inpatient unit where I worked for many years, I usually gave the median as well as the mean, because the distribution is skewed. The median length of stay is usually about a month, while the mean is four to six months because of a few long-term patients; the fact that more than half the patients are discharged in about a month describes the population better than the mean does. The median is the commonly used measure of central tendency for reporting the price of homes, because it is less affected by the small number of extremely expensive homes than is the mean. The median gives a more meaningful value than the mean would give in this situation because it reflects better what most people are typically paying for homes, without being influenced by the few expensive homes that skew the distribution.

Mode

The **mode** is the most frequent score. There may be more than one mode in a distribution. Suppose ten people took a ten-point quiz and had these scores:

Score	f (frequency)
10	1
9	3
8	2
7	3
5	1

Learning Key

Mean: Arithmetic average; found by adding all the values and dividing by the number of cases; used only with interval data.

Median: Middle number in a group of ranked numbers; the fiftieth percentile; appropriate average for ordinal measurement or skewed interval distributions.

Mode: Most frequently observed number or score; only average available for nominal measurement.

Normal curve: Theoretically perfect frequency distribution, in which the mean, median and mode are all the same and which takes the form of a symmetrical bell-shaped curve.

We would have two modes: 9 and 7. The mode is the *only* measure one can use with nominal measurements. We can identify the modal, or most frequently occurring, type or types in a personality type table, but we cannot find a mean or median type because the types are nominal measurement.

In a normal distribution, the mean, median, and mode will all be the same. That is one of the defining characteristics of the **normal curve**, a theoretically perfect, bell-shaped frequency distribution with the mean, median, and mode all coinciding at the center. Note in figure 2.2 that in a negatively skewed distribution, the mean is lower than the median. In a positive skew, the mean is higher than the median.

The calculation of the mean, median, and mode is illustrated in table 2.3 which takes a group of 10 of the height measurements from table 2.1.

TABLE 2.3
Measures of Central Tendency of Heights of 10 Eight-Year-Olds

Height (X)		
46	Mean	= $\dfrac{\text{Sum of } (\sum) \text{ observations}}{\text{Number (N) of observations}}$
48		
49		$\overline{X} = \dfrac{\sum X}{N} = \dfrac{500}{10} = 50$
49		
50		
50	Median	= middle score = 50
51		(halfway between the
52		two 50's)
52	Mode	= most frequent observation
53		= 49, 50, 52
500		(each occurs twice)

Measures of Variability

Distributions differ not only in where their center is, but in how much spread or dispersion there is around the central point. The most common measures of variability are the range and standard deviation.

Overview

The simplest measure of variability is the **range**, the difference between the highest and lowest scores. The range is used with interval data when a quick and rough estimate of variability is needed, or when extremes are important. In most cases extreme scores are not most important, and then the range has limited usefulness because it is based on extreme scores. The *interquartile range*, which describes the middle 50% of the scores, is sometimes used to show variability without as great an impact from extreme scores.

The most widely used measure of variability with interval data is the **standard deviation (SD)**, which is a standard measure of how spread out the individual scores are around the mean and is based on the deviations between each score and the mean of the distribution. If a distribution is reasonably normal, the distribution can be reconstructed by knowing the mean and the SD. The exact percentage of cases that will be included in any given number of standard deviations above or below the mean can be found in tables in many statistics books.

Another measure of variability is the **variance**, found by squaring the standard deviation. The variance is a measure of all the scatter of scores in a distribution, and is valuable because it can conveniently be partitioned into component parts.

Z-scores are **standard scores** that are used when one needs to compare performance on two or more different tests. Z-scores use standard deviations to convert scores from different tests into a universal language of standard deviation units. **T-scores** and stanine scores are other standard scores formed from the basic z-score. They help us avoid negative numbers.

Centile, or *percentile, scores* also help make comparisons among individuals and tests. A centile score tells the percentage of scores falling at or below a particular score in a distribution. They are useful when a distribution is skewed, when we can't assume we have interval measurements, or when we are talking to lay people who may be confused by standard scores.

Measures of central tendency tell us where the center of a distribution is. Different distributions have different center points. Distributions also differ from one another in their variability—the spread or dispersion of scores around the central point. In our example of eight-year-olds, the children do not all have the same height even though they are all the same age. There is variability, or variance, in their heights.

Measures of variability provide us with a description of thè relative spread of the scores, whether the distribution is wide or slender. Figure 2.6 shows two normal distributions with the same mean and median, but one is wider, and the other is more slender.

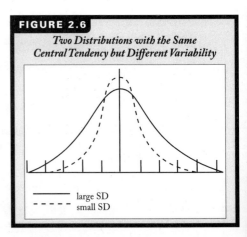

FIGURE 2.6

Two Distributions with the Same Central Tendency but Different Variability

——— large SD
- - - - small SD

Range

The simplest measure of variability is the **range**. This is the difference between the highest and lowest scores. In table 2.3, we would subtract the lowest score (46) from the highest (53), giving us a difference or range of 7. We could also say, "The range is from 46 to 53." Giving the actual top and bottom scores is often more meaningful than just stating the difference between them.

The range is best used with interval data. It is based only on extreme scores—the highest and lowest individual scores—so a change in one of these extremes directly changes the size of the range, even if most of our scores are in the middle of the distribution, far away from the extremes. Therefore, it is generally not very valuable. Statisticians use the range only when a very quick and very crude estimate of variability is needed. In some instances, however, the range can be quite useful. If you ask me about the weather in Nebraska in March as you prepare to come for a visit, knowing the mean daily temperature will not be sufficient information. Knowing the range will help you come prepared for the possibility of either the very cold or the quite balmy days we often have that month.

Some researchers use a special kind of range, called the *interquartile range*, which describes the middle 50% of the scores. The bottom 25% and top 25% of the scores are not counted. The middle 50% contains half of the cases while ignoring the extreme scores that can have such a large impact on the range. This is the most frequently reported measure of variability when the median is used.

Standard Deviation

The most useful measure of variability with interval data is the **standard deviation**. It is the one most frequently used by behavioral scientists. The abbreviation SD is used for standard deviation. It may also be shown in either capital or lowercase letters.

The standard deviation is based on the differences, or deviations, between each score and the arithmetic mean of the distribution. Deviations are found by subtracting the mean from each score. Calculating the deviations of all the

---

Learning Key

Range: Distance between the lowest and highest scores; the simplest measure of variability.

Standard deviation: Most common measure of variability, showing how spread out individual scores in a distribution are around the mean; based on deviations from the mean; a normal distribution can be reconstructed knowing only the mean and SD.

individual scores gives us some positive and some negative numbers. When we add together all these deviations, we get a sum of zero. One definition of the mean is based on an understanding of deviations. The mean is the balance point in a distribution, the point around which all the deviations add up to zero.

The standard deviation is a measure of the scatter of the scores. When the deviation of scores from the mean is large, the SD is also large. When the deviations are small, the SD is correspondingly small.

Table 2.4, column 1 presents the same data used in table 2.3. The first score is 46 and the mean is 50. The deviation of this first score is -4. Deviations from the mean of all column 1 entries are in column 2. Note that these deviations add up to zero, and so do not themselves provide a measure of variability. We could get around this problem of the deviations adding to zero by taking absolute deviations (ignoring the + or -), but the better way is to square them.

To compute the standard deviation, we square each of the deviations, add them up, divide by the number of deviations, and finally take the square root of the resulting number. Thus the standard deviation is the root-mean-square of the deviations of measurements from their arithmetic mean.

$$SD = \sqrt{\frac{\Sigma\, x^2}{N}}$$

TABLE 2.4

Calculating Variability in Heights of Eight-Year-Olds

(1) Height	(2) Deviation	(3) Deviation squared	(4) Standard score
X	x	x^2	z_x
46	-4	16	-2.0
48	-2	4	-1.0
49	-1	1	-0.5
49	-1	1	-0.5
50	0	0	0.0
50	0	0	0.0
51	1	1	+0.5
52	2	4	+1.0
52	2	4	+1.0
53	3	9	+1.5
	0	40	

$$\text{Standard deviation} = \sqrt{\frac{\Sigma\, x^2}{N}} = \sqrt{\frac{40}{10}} = \sqrt{4} = 2$$

This process is illustrated in column 3 of table 2.4. We square each of the deviations before adding them together; then we take the square root of the mean (total divided by N). Note that the capital X denotes a raw score, while the lower case x represents a deviation from the mean of the X scores. The Greek letter sigma (Σ) is the symbol for *sum of.*

Some readers who are acquainted with statistics will be familiar with a different formula for finding the standard deviation. To keep our example simple, we are using the formula for a population standard deviation here so we can save an explanation of degrees of freedom until later. Don't worry about understanding any of those terms yet. Suffice it to say that most formulas for the standard deviation divide the sum of squared deviations by N - 1 rather than N.

Why all the trouble, this squaring and taking square roots? Squaring helps get rid of negative numbers, but the most important reason is that the standard deviation has superior mathematical properties over using absolute deviations. The SD is such a good measure of variability that, if the frequency distribution is reasonably normal, the distribution can be reconstructed by knowing two numbers, the mean and the SD, as shown in figure 2.7. The SD can be used as a measuring tape to mark off units along the measurement scale of our distribution.

You may never need to calculate a standard deviation. However, you will frequently encounter SDs in test manuals and research literature, and so you will need to understand this concept: The standard deviation is a standard measure of how spread out the individual scores in a distribution are around the mean.

Percentages in a Distribution

We noted earlier that the SD is such a good measure of variability that, if the distribution is reasonably normal, the distribution can be approximated by knowing only two numbers, the mean and the SD. The exact percentage of cases that will be included in any given number of standard deviations above or below the mean is known from tables that have been constructed using the formula of the normal curve. The information we can find in such tables, readily

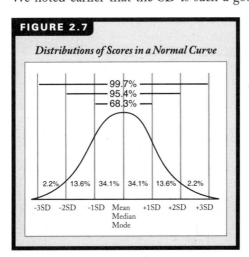

FIGURE 2.7

Distributions of Scores in a Normal Curve

99.7%
95.4%
68.3%

2.2% 13.6% 34.1% 34.1% 13.6% 2.2%

-3SD -2SD -1SD Mean +1SD +2SD +3SD
Median
Mode

available from statistics books and other sources, is summarized and simplified in figure 2.7.

We know, for example, that 68.3% of cases in a normal distribution will fall between -1 SD and +1 SD (34.15% in the SD below the mean and 34.15% in the SD above the mean). We can see that 2.2% of the cases will fall between +2 SD and +3 SD. Statistics books have tables showing the percentage of cases that will fall between any fraction of a standard deviation and the mean in a normal distribution. These predictable percentages in areas under the normal curve will be particularly important to us a bit later when we consider inferential statistics and need to estimate how likely it is that a particular result could have happened just by chance.

Variance

In the process of calculating the standard deviation, we come to another measure of the spread of the scores, called the **variance**. Like the SD, the variance is a measure of the scatter in a distribution. The variance is the sum of the squared deviations, divided by N—what we had in our formula before we took the square root to get the SD. The variance is the standard deviation squared, SD^2.

The variance is useful because it measures everything that is happening in a set of data—including both the differences in the variables we are studying and all sources of error. The variance is important because it can be conveniently *partitioned*, or divided up into component parts, as we will see later in our consideration of correlation and in the test of significance called *analysis of variance* (often abbreviated ANOVA).

The variance is not as helpful in describing the spread in a distribution as the SD is, because the variance is not in the same unit of measurement as our data. If our data are in inches, the SD will be in inches, but the variance (SD^2) will be in inches that have been squared.

As we saw when we discussed measures of central tendency, we can have several statistics that relate to the same general concept, but each in a different way. Mean, median, and mode all describe the center point of a distribution, but each describes something different, and we cannot use them interchangeably. The measures of variability—range, SD, variance—all describe the spread of scores, but each in a different way.

If we want to describe the variability of the heights of our eight-year-olds, we will use the standard deviation, because standard deviation units are in the same units as our original data. We measured the heights in inches, and the standard deviation is in inches. We would not use the variance, because we are not interested in showing the variability in heights in inches that have been squared.

That is not part of our usual experience and understanding. However, when we are doing an experiment with heights, the variance may be helpful as we try to determine how large the relationship is between height and another variable, or whether relationships with height are larger than we could have expected by chance alone. As with all statistics, we choose the measure that is most effective in doing what we need to show or do.

Z-scores, T-scores, and Centile Scores

One important use of the standard deviation is to help us convert scores from different types of measures into standard scores, a universal language of standard deviation units. Suppose you took a variety of vocational aptitude tests, but each one had a different number of possible points, and a different mean and standard deviation. How would you know whether your score of 103 on the mechanical aptitude test is better than your score of 62 on the music test? You convert both to **z-scores** by subtracting the mean of the norm group on each test from your score on that test, and dividing each deviation by the SD of that test. Then you have scores that can be directly compared; each would tell you how many standard deviations above or below the mean you were on each of the tests.

To illustrate, we find the **z-score** for the tallest child in table 2.4 by subtracting the mean (50) from that child's height (53) and dividing by the standard deviation (2).

$$\text{z-score} = \frac{\text{score - arithmetic mean}}{\text{standard deviation}}$$
$$= (53 - 50) \div 2 = 1.5$$

In other words, the tallest child has a z-score of 1.5 and is 1.5 SD above the mean. Similarly, the shortest child has a z-score of -2.0 and is 2 standard deviations below the mean.

$$(46 - 50) \div 2 = -2.0$$

When we convert our scores to z-scores, we have a distribution with a mean of 0 and a standard deviation of 1. Z-scores put numbers from different distributions into a new language of standard deviation units, so we are able to compare them, even though the original measurements from which they came (such as inches and pounds) were not comparable.

Another way to think of this is to imagine we have a set of measurements, some of which are in inches and some of which are in centimeters. We can't combine or compare them until they are in the same language, either English or metric. If we converted the English into metric, or the metric into English units, we could directly compare. Alternatively, we could convert both into a third measurement language so they would be in the same units of measurement.

Myers used z-scores when she conducted studies in twenty-five medical schools to test a hypothesis that students with certain personality types had an academic advantage over students with other personality types. Different medical schools used different scales for reporting grade point averages. To use GPA to test hypotheses about type and academic advantage, she needed to convert the individual student GPAs into z-scores. Z-scores gave relative class rank for each student, and this was directly comparable across schools.

Z-scores are sometimes called **standard scores** or standardized scores. Other standard scores may be formed from the basic z-score. One reason we may want to use a different standard score is that in a normal distribution, half of our measurements will be below the mean, so half of our z-scores will be negative. Negative numbers can be unhandy, so we can convert z-scores to other standard scores. The **T-score** is commonly used with many psychological tests, such as the Minnesota Multiphasic Personality Inventory (MMPI), and has the advantage of always being a positive number. To obtain a T-score, multiply each z-score by 10 and then add 50. Since we multiply by 10 to create a T-score, we also avoid the decimal points typically used with z-scores. With z-scores, we know directly how many standard deviations the individual score falls above or below the mean; $z = -1.0$ is one standard deviation below the mean and $z = 0.5$ is one-half standard deviation above the mean. With T-scores, the mean is 50 and the standard deviation is 10, so a $T = 60$ is one standard deviation above the mean and a $T = 30$ is two standard deviations below the mean on that test.

A *centile* score is another way to make comparisons among individuals and tests. A centile score is the percentage of scores falling at or below a particular person's score in the distribution. If a person had a centile score of 85, we would know that 85% of the scores in the distribution fall at or below this person's score. If we have a group of 20 scores, 17 scores would fall below the 85th centile; if we

---

Learning Key

Variance: Measure of variability that can be partitioned into component parts; it is SD^2.

Z-score or standard score: Tells how far above or below the mean any given score is in standard deviation units; allows conversion of numbers from different distributions into a common language of standard deviation units. **T-score:** a standard score created by multiplying z-scores by 10 and adding 50, so pluses or minuses and decimal points are not needed.

have a group of 500 scores, 425 would fall below this centile.

Centile scores, also called *percentile scores*, are useful when a distribution is badly skewed or if we can't assume we have a distribution of interval measurements. Centile scores are also useful when we are talking to people who don't understand standard deviations, z-scores and T-scores. Lay people have a better idea what percentiles mean. When we are dealing with ordinal measurements—or interval measurements in a distribution that is not symmetrical—the easiest way to indicate variability is to state the 25th, 50th and 75th percentile points, that is, the median and the interquartile range. Figure 2.8 compares z-scores, T-scores, and centile scores.

Another standard score, used with some educational tests, is the *stanine* or standard nine, which is approximated by multiplying the z-score by 2 and adding 5. Actually, stanines divide the normal curve into nine intervals ranging from 1 to 9, with a mean of 5. To convert a z-score to a stanine requires that the z-score first be converted to a percentile, then converted to a stanine using these percentages: Stanines 1 and 9 contain the bottom and top 4 % of cases, stanines 2 and 8 contain the next 7%, 3 and 7 contain 12%, 4 and 6 contain 17%, and stanine 5 contains 20%. In actual practice, stanines are likely to be found with a computer program or a conversion table.

FIGURE 2.8

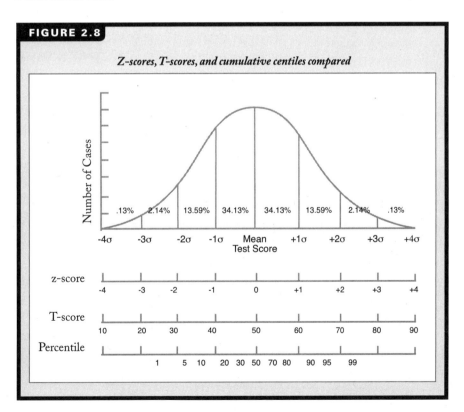

Z-scores, T-scores, and cumulative centiles compared

27

Correlation

Correlation is a way to look at the co-relationship between two variables. To what extent do two things go together? As scores on one variable increase, do scores on the other variable also increase—or do they decrease?

Overview

Scatter plots provide a visual picture of the degree and nature of a correlation. When a correlation is zero, the points on the scatter diagram are randomly distributed and do not line up in any particular direction. If the correlation is moderate, the scatter narrows in one direction or another. If the correlation is perfect, the scatter diagram is a straight line. Positive correlations slope from lower left to upper right and negative correlations slope from upper left to lower right.

The **correlation coefficient** is a measure of the relationship between two variables and has two parts. The degree of correlation is expressed by a number between 0.00 and 1.00. The direction of the relationship is indicated by a sign, plus or minus. What matters most is the degree of the relationship; the direction typically is no surprise. In positive correlations, high scores on one measure are associated with high scores on the other measure, and low scores with low scores. In negative correlations, high scores on one measure are associated with low scores on the other measure, and low scores with high scores.

The most common measure of correlation, used when both variables are measured on an interval scale, is the Pearson product-moment correlation coefficient, which has the symbol r. A high positive Pearson r indicates that each individual in a distribution has approximately the same z-score on both variables. With a high negative correlation, each individual has approximately the same z-score on both variables, but the z-scores are opposite in sign.

A variety of other kinds of correlation are used when one or both measures are not interval data. Correlation coefficients exist for every combination of level of measurement. Even though these other correlations are calculated differently, the resulting coefficient is similar in meaning and use to the Pearson r.

Correlation is not causation. A correlation simply tells us that individual differences in two sets of measurements tend to vary together, not necessarily that one causes the other. When there is a high correlation, typically both sets of differences are caused by some common factors.

Correlation coefficients look like percents, but they are not. A correlation coefficient tells us the extent to which the variables are related, but not in a way that is common for us. In **variance accounted for**, we are converting correlations to percents, asking what percentage of all the effects in the two distributions that we have correlated is directly attributable to the relationship between the two variables. To find the variance accounted for, we square the correlation coefficient. Squaring the correlation coefficient converts the correlation into a percentage. Squaring correlation coefficients whenever we see them helps us understand literature about psychological assessment tools. Many reliability and validity correlations look good, but the degree of relationship appears less substantial when the correlation is squared, and we get the smaller percentage figure.

So far we've been talking about frequency distributions considered one at a time. However, much of science is concerned with co-relations between two or more distributions of measurements. To help us see what correlation means, let's consider the two variables of height and weight. We know from observation that people differ a lot in height and in weight. We can take any group of people and find their average heights and average weights. We can also measure the variability of their heights and the variability of their weights.

But we know also that there must be a relationship—a correlation—between height and weight. In general, people who are tall weigh more than those who are short. Obviously the correlation is not perfect, for some people who are 5 feet tall weigh more than some who are 6 feet tall. So correlation is a matter of degree.

Scatter plots

One of the clearest ways to show the meaning of the concept of correlation is graphically, in the form of a scatter plot or scatter diagram. In the construction of such graphs, the X (horizontal) axis represents one of the correlated measures and the Y (vertical) axis represents the other. Each dot in a scatter plot represents one individual, and the dot is at the intersection of the person's score on the horizontally-plotted variable with the person's score on the vertically-plotted variable. In a scatter plot, low scores on each variable are in the lower left-hand corner of the graph. To illustrate, let's plot the relationship between the height and weight for our 10 children from table 2.4 (see page 22), using the following data.

Height and weight of 10 children

Height (inches)	46	48	49	49	50	50	51	52	52	53
Weight (pounds)	51	48	47	56	57	55	54	58	63	61

Scatter plots provide a visual picture of the degree of a correlation because the amount of scatter, and its direction, varies with the correlation. When there is no correlation, the points on the scatter diagram are randomly distributed and do not line up in any particular direction. If the correlation is moderate, as in our figure 2.9, the scatter narrows in one direction or another. If the correlation is perfect, the scatter diagram is a straight line. Figure 2.10 illustrates this, as well as a moderate and a nearly zero correlation.

Scatter plots not only help us see the direction and degree (or strength) of a relationship, but can also show us the nature of a relationship, as illustrated in figure 2.11. Suppose two variables were correlated, but only for high scores on each variable; in this case, we would expect a random scattering of dots in the lower left corner of the plot, but a clear relationship shown in the upper right corner, as we see in the first graph in figure 2.11. Or suppose we were correlating amount of anxiety and school test performance. We would probably find a *curvilinear* relationship, with increasing anxiety from very low to moderate being associated with improving test performance. But once we are past moderate anxiety,

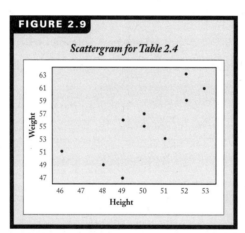

FIGURE 2.9

Scattergram for Table 2.4

headed for very high anxiety, test scores are apt to go down as anxiety rises. We would expect the dots in the scatter plot to look like a sideways U, as we see in the second graph in figure 2.11. In this case, the correlation would be near zero, even though the variables are strongly related, because the product-moment correlation is a measure of *linear* (straight-line) relationship.

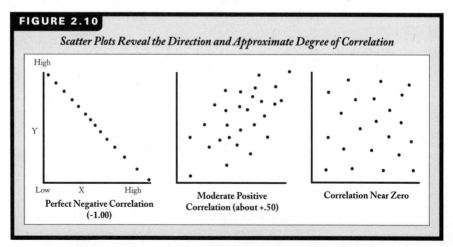

FIGURE 2.10

Scatter Plots Reveal the Direction and Approximate Degree of Correlation

Perfect Negative Correlation
(-1.00)

Moderate Positive
Correlation (about +.50)

Correlation Near Zero

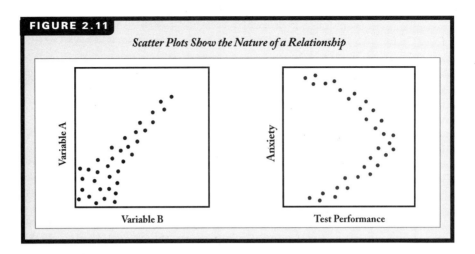

FIGURE 2.11

Scatter Plots Show the Nature of a Relationship

Pearson r

While scatter plots provide a visual picture of the concept of correlation, they are not an efficient way to report correlation. In a report or a table, we report the relationship between variables through a number, called a **correlation coefficient**. The correlation coefficient has two parts, one showing the degree of the correlation—how much relationship there is—and the other showing the direction of the relationship—which way the relationship goes. The *degree* of correlation is expressed by a number between 0.00 and 1.00. Zero represents no correlation at all, while 1.00 represents a perfect correlation. If we correlated measurements of a set of objects in inches with measurements of the same objects in centimeters, we'd have a perfect correlation of 1.00.

Our major concern is generally with the degree of the relationship in a correlation. However, we also want to know the *direction* of the relationship. We use a sign, + (plus) or - (minus), to indicate direction. If high scores on one variable go with high scores on the other variable, or if low scores on one go with low scores on the other, then we have a positive correlation and use the + sign. On the other hand, if high scores on one variable go with low scores on the other variable, we have a negative correlation and use a minus sign (-) before our correlation number.

Because the degree of relationship is most important, we look first at the number rather than the sign. A correlation coefficient of -.63 is larger than a coefficient of +.54.

When we do look at the sign, we are likely to notice that there is arbitrariness about whether the relationship we have found is positive or negative. For example, if we correlate scores of an Extraversion–Introversion scale on the MBTI instrument with scores on a sociability scale, it doesn't really make any difference whether high scores indicate sociability or being reserved, there is a relationship. As a matter of fact, which end of a scale has which meaning is a decision of the test developer. Myers made Introversion the high end of her Extraversion–Introversion scale, but many other tests of this dimension have Extraversion on the high end.

The direction of the relationship typically is no surprise. We expect that Extraversion will correlate with sociability, and that Introversion will correlate with being reserved, even though the relationships will not be large because Extraversion and Introversion are much more than those characteristics. We aren't expecting an upset in what most observers have come to expect. Instead, we are looking for the amount or degree of relationship between these variables. The issue of whether the relationship will be positive or negative depends on how we have phrased our question or which end of a dimension a test developer has coded for high scores.

The most common measure of correlation, used when measurements on both variables are on an interval scale, is the *Pearson product-moment correlation coefficient*, which has the symbol r, or sometimes R. A high positive Pearson r indicates that individuals in a group or distribution have approximately the same z-score on both variables. With a high negative correlation, individuals have approximately the same z-score on both variables, but the z-scores are opposite in sign (one is + and the other is -).

The fact that Johnny has a z-score on X of +2 and a z-score on Y of +1.95 does not itself make a correlation, but the fact that similar z-scores on X and Y are received by the whole group makes the correlation. Billy's z_x of -1 is similar to his z_y of -1.2 and Mary's z_x of .2 is similar to her z_y of .15. When Billy's and Mary's scores are put together with Johnny's scores in a distribution, the pattern in the group creates the correlation or relationship between the two variables. Or if we were studying the relationship between water temperature and the growth of algae in aquariums, it would not be the fact that we had a low level of algae at a low temperature that creates the correlation, but the fact that moderate

---

Learning Key

Correlation coefficient: Measures the degree of relationship between two variables, ranging from 0.00 (no correlation) to 1.00 (perfect correlation); the sign (+ or-) tells the direction of the relationship, with + meaning that high scores on one variable go with high scores on the other variable, and - meaning that high scores on one variable go with low scores on the other variable; size of the number is usually more important than the sign.

Variance accounted for: Converting a correlation to a percentage by squaring the correlation coefficient; tells the percentage of the differences within the two correlated variables that is directly related to the relationship between the two variables.

temperature and moderate algae growth go together, as do higher temperature and higher algae growth.

To better understand the correlation coefficient, it may be helpful to look at the formula and a calculation example. To find a Pearson r, we multiply each individual z-score on the X-variable times the individual z-score on the Y-variable. We then add up all these z-score cross-products and divide by N. The formula for the Pearson r is

$$r = \frac{\sum (z_x z_y)}{N}$$

$$\text{Pearson } r = \frac{\text{sum of (X z-score times Y z-score) for all cases,}}{\text{divided by the number of cases}}$$

Calculation of a Pearson r is illustrated in table 2.5. The z-scores for height (column 2) are the same as we calculated in table 2.4. The z-scores for weight are calculated in the same way, subtracting the mean of all the weights (55) from each obtained weight and dividing by the standard deviation of the weights (5). We then multiply each child's height z-score times his or her weight z-score (see values in column 5 of table 2.5), add them up (7.6) and divide by N (10), and we find a correlation coefficient of .76.

We would read this finding as "The correlation between height and weight in 8-year-olds is point seven six."

TABLE 2.5

Correlating Height and Weight of 10 Eight-Year Olds

(1) Height	(2) Standard score	(3) Weight	(4) Standard score	(5) z cross-products
X	z_x	Y	z_y	$z_x z_y$
46	-2.0	51	-0.8	1.6
48	-1.0	48	-1.4	1.4
49	-0.5	47	-1.6	0.8
49	-0.5	56	0.2	-0.1
50	0.0	57	0.4	0.0
50	0.0	55	0.0	0.0
51	0.5	54	-0.2	-0.1
52	1.0	58	0.6	0.6
52	1.0	63	1.6	1.6
53	1.5	61	1.2	1.8
500		550		7.6

$\overline{X} = 50; \ SD_x = 2; \ \overline{Y} = 55; \ SD_y = 5; \ Pearson\ r = .76$

As you look at the values in column 5, you can see that when the X and Y z-scores have the same sign, the result of multiplying them together (the cross-product) will be positive. If the z-scores have different signs, the resulting cross-product will be negative. When some of the cross-products are different in sign from most of the others, the total sum of cross-products and the degree of correlation are reduced. For some simpler ways to calculate Pearson r, see "Alternate Formulas" (page 41).

The Pearson product-moment correlation coefficient, the most frequent correlation coefficient in behavioral science, is used when both measures are interval measurements. Correlation is possible for *any* two sets of measurements, whether they are nominal, ordinal, interval, or any combination of these. "Other Kinds of Correlation" (page 42) explains several different correlation coefficients, all of which are similar in meaning and use to the Pearson r.

Correlation is not Causation

Sometimes people infer that if two things are correlated, one must be causing the other, but that usually is *not* the case. When there is a correlation, both sets of individual differences are usually caused by some common factors. In our height and weight example, we cannot say a person's height causes weight, or that weight causes height, for both height and weight are caused by individual differences in genetic inheritance, nutrition, and so forth. *A correlation simply tells us that individual differences in two sets of measurements tend to vary together, not necessarily that one causes the other.*

There is a fairly high correlation between monthly ice cream sales and number of homicides in New York City. It seems unlikely that ice cream sales cause murder or that murder rates create a market for ice cream sales. The correlation is undoubtedly caused by the fact that warm weather makes both ice cream sales and homicides more likely. In this case, we would call the weather a lurking variable, something other than the variables we are correlating that account for the relationship.

While correlation does not mean causation, we can sometimes infer something about causation from correlational information. However, to decide which is cause and which is effect requires a large number of correlations and careful logical analysis. For example, the Centers for Disease Control use correlations in determining that a particular virus causes a particular disease, but it takes many correlations, some large and some negligible, in a complicated process to establish that the virus is the cause.

Variance Accounted For

Correlation coefficients look like percents, but *correlation coefficients are not percents.*

While a correlation coefficient measures the relationship between two distributions or variables, it does not tell us the extent to which they are related in a way that is common in our thinking. If they were stated in terms of percentages, we would understand them readily.

Fortunately we have a way to translate a correlation coefficient into a percentage, by using **variance accounted for**, sometimes also called *variance explained* or *coefficient of determination*. In variance accounted for we are asking the following:

- what percentage of the variance in one measure is *predicted* by the variance in the other measure?

or

- what percentage of all the effects in the two distributions is directly attributable to the relationship between the two variables?

To find the variance accounted for, we square the correlation coefficient. *Variance accounted for, which is the squared correlation coefficient, r^2, provides us with a measure of the meaningfulness of a correlation, expressed in percentage terms.* In symbols, variance accounted for is $r^2 = \%$.

In our example of children's heights and weights, we found a correlation coefficient of .76. If you look at table 2.5 (page 33), you will note that not all the children have the same height. These differences create variance. Because their weights differed as well, there is also variance in the children's weights. So we may want to know how differences in height can be predicted by our knowledge of weight, or weight predicted by knowledge of height. We get that answer by squaring the correlation coefficient. In this case,

$$.76 \times .76 = .58.$$

This tells us that 58% of the variability in our sample can be accounted for by the relationship between height and weight, and 42% is related to other factors.

Earlier we considered the sentence, "The correlation between height and weight in eight-year-olds is .76." When we understand variance accounted for, we know that although the number in the sentence looks like a percent, it is not. We know that to find meaning in the number, we must square the correlation coefficient to find variance accounted for. Then we can mentally translate the sentence to read, "The percent of relationship between height and weight in eight-year-olds is 58%."

When the relationship is not perfect (r is less than 1.00), we know there are other factors in our measures besides the co-relationship between our two variables. In our height and weight example, variance *not* accounted for could have been the result of factors such as genetics, malnutrition, obesity, bone structure, chance, and so forth. In addition, it could have been noise in our measurements, such as our scales or tape measure not being perfect or because of errors we made in recording the measurements we took.

The Venn diagram in figure 2.12 presents another way of looking at variance accounted for. The circle containing X represents all the variability or variance (differences among scores) of the X variable, and the other circle represents the total variance of Y. The overlapping (shaded) area indicates their shared variance; this overlapping area is what r^2 shows us.

Squaring correlation coefficients helps us understand literature about psychological assessment tools. Many relationships between scores on one instrument and other measurements appear substantial, but we need to be aware of variance *unaccounted for*, and thus we need to be modest in our assertions. There may be a highly significant correlation of .40 between the Intuition preference on the Sensing–Intuition dichotomy of the MBTI instrument and the psychologist scale on a career interest inventory, but before I feel out of place being a psychologist with a Sensing preference, I need to recall that the relationship only accounts for 16% (.40 x .40 = .16) of the variance, and 84% is related to other things.

Correlations in the .70s and .80s are considered to be very good in the behavioral sciences. However, we need to be aware that correlations this large only account for 50% to 75% of the variance, and anywhere from 25% to 50% of the variance in such correlations may be accounted for by other factors.

Variance accounted for is the percentage of all the effects in two distributions we have correlated that is directly attributable to the relationship between the two variables. Or more simply, remember that *correlation coefficients are not percents, but squaring a correlation coefficient converts it into a percentage.*

The reliability and validity information in most test manuals consists largely of correlation data. You don't need to memorize the formulas or calculate correlations, but to read the information in tables, you will need to know what a correlation is, what r stands for, and the fact that you will need to square the correlation coefficient to know how large the relationship is in percentage terms.

We have seen several ways descriptive statistics help us summarize data: in frequency distributions, in showing where the center is and how spread out the scores are, and in measuring the degree and direction of relationship between variables. We are now ready to see how statistics help us know whether differences we find can be generalized.

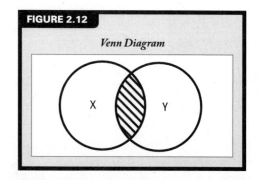

FIGURE 2.12

Venn Diagram

Exercises and Questions to Check Your Understanding

1. Frequency distributions are a way of summarizing data. Which of the following are *frequency distributions?*

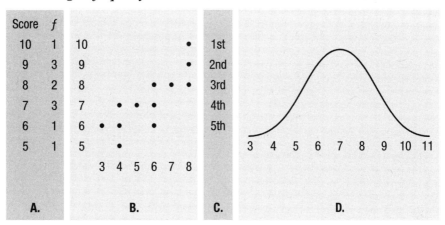

Score	f
10	1
9	3
8	2
7	3
6	1
5	1

A.   B.   C.   D.

2. Often the choice of which particular statistic we use will depend on the level of measurement our data is in. Check your understanding of levels of measurement. Match the following kinds of data we have collected with the type of measurement represented.

   a. nominal   b. ordinal   c. interval only   d. ratio

   ___ A. miles of highway

   ___ B. finishers in a stock-car race, listed in order of finish

   ___ C. inventory of a hardware store, with numbers of shovels, hoes, rakes, etc.

   ___ D. scores on an academic achievement test

3. Put these numbers in rank order: 3, 9, 2, 4, 7, 4, 5, 4, 7

   ___ ___ ___ ___ ___ ___ ___ ___ ___

   Find: A. the mean _____

   B. the median _____

   C. the mode _____

   D. the range _____

37

4. **A group of students is given a quiz. The mean for the group is 60 and the SD is 8.**

    A. What are the z-scores for each of the following quiz scores?

    B. Using Figure 2.8 on page 27, what is an approximate percentile for each?

Quiz score	72	44	62
A. z-score	____	____	____
B. percentile	____	____	____

    C. What range of scores would fall between -1.5 SD and +1.5 SD? ____

5. **A school gives a variety of vocational aptitude tests to its students and finds these results:**

	N	X̄	SD
Mechanical aptitude	172	110	15
Musical aptitude	185	54	8

    A. Identify each of these symbols:

        1) N _____

        2) X̄ _____

        3) SD _____

    B. Here are two normal curves, one for a mechanical aptitude test and one for a musical aptitude test. Mark the scores that would fall at each standard deviation for each test.

Mechanical

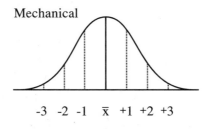

    -3 -2 -1   x̄   +1 +2 +3

Musical

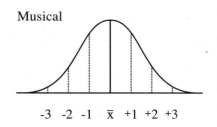

    -3 -2 -1   x̄   +1 +2 +3

    C. Johnny took these tests and received scores of 103 on the mechanical aptitude test and 62 on the music test. For each test, approximate Johnny's score as a z-score:

        1) Mechanical _____

        2) Musical _____

D. Mark an x on each normal curve to indicate Johnny's z-score.

E. On which test did Johnny have the higher score? _____

F. Assuming mechanical aptitude scores are normally distributed, between what two scores on this test would about 95% of students be expected to fall?

between _____ and _____

6. Don't compute it, but examine this data.

Group X   20,   22,   23,   24,   24,   26,   27

Group Y   14,   18,   19,   21,   24,   28,   31

A. Which of these groups would have the larger SD? _____

B. If everyone in a group had the same score, what would the SD be?

_____

7. For each pair of correlation coefficients below, circle the larger one.

A. -.63 or +.17

B. -.42 or +.53

C. -.72 or +.65

8. Each of these hypotheses expects the same relationship between coffee consumption and sleep. Mark a + (plus) by the correlations you would expect to be positive and a − (minus) by the correlations you would expect to be negative.

____ A. As number of cups of coffee consumed increases, number of hours of lost sleep increases.

____ B. As number of cups of coffee consumed decreases, number of hours of lost sleep decreases.

____ C. As number of cups of coffee consumed increases, number of hours of sleep decreases.

9. Describe the relationship between the two variables plotted on each scattergram.

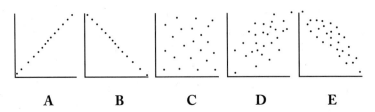

A   B   C   D   E

A. _____

B. _____

C. _____

D. _____

E. _____

10. Identify (name) these symbols:

A. r _____

B. r^2 _____

11. To convert a correlation coefficient to a percentage, we need to: _____

_____ .

12. How much variance is accounted for by each of these correlation coefficients?

A. $r = .40$ _____

B. $r = -.50$ _____

C. $r = .75$ _____

Alternate Formulas

For most any of the statistics we have considered, there are alternate formulas which statisticians have proven are algebraically equivalent. We are able to choose the one that is easiest to use, given the nature of our data.

$$r = \frac{\sum (z_x z_y)}{N}$$

Z-score formula. The Pearson product-moment correlation coefficient was introduced with a formula based on z-scores. We multiply each individual's X z-score times that person's Y z-score, add up these cross products and divide by N, the number of individuals. This formula is helpful in understanding the Pearson r conceptually, but it would not be an easy formula to use with some data because we'd have to calculate means, standard deviations, and z scores first before we carried out the multiplying of cross-products. For calculating a correlation coefficient directly from raw scores and deviations, we can use either of two formulas, which are algebraically equivalent to our z-score formula.

$$r = \frac{\sum xy}{\sqrt{\sum x^2 \cdot y^2}}$$

Deviations formula. The first of these would be handy if we had deviations from the X mean and the Y mean for each individual. In this formula, we would multiply each individual's deviation from the X mean times that individual's deviation from the Y mean, and sum these across all individuals. We then divide this total by the square root of the summed x deviations squared times the summed y deviations squared.

$$r = \frac{\dfrac{\sum XY - \overline{X}\overline{Y}}{N}}{SD_x\, SD_y}$$

Raw scores, means, and SDs formula. Another formula uses raw scores plus the means and standard deviations of X and Y, so would be the easiest to apply, because reports of data that have been collected typically include information about means and standard deviations. In this formula, the sum of the X score times the Y score for each individual is divided by the number of individuals; the X mean is multiplied times the Y mean, and this is subtracted from the first result; this new result is divided by the standard deviation of the X variable times the standard deviation of the Y variable.

You won't need to memorize any of these formulas; they are presented here only to illustrate the fact that in statistics there is often more than one way to accomplish the same thing. We can use the formula that is most convenient given the nature of the data we have.

Other Kinds of Correlation

When we don't have interval measurement, there are other correlation coefficients that are calculated differently and have some different statistical properties, but are similar in meaning and character to the Pearson product-moment correlation. The following are four other correlation coefficients.

The *Rank-difference correlation*, or rho, is used if we have ordinal measurement instead of interval measurement. For example, we might correlate individuals' class ranks and ranks in amount of scholarship aid received.

Biserial correlation is used when one of the two variables being correlated is on an interval scale and the other scale is dichotomous—it has only two values, like true and false, pass and fail, Extraversion and Introversion. An example would be correlating grade point average (on an interval scale) and gender (dichotomous).

The *Phi coefficient* is used when both variables are scored dichotomously, and when they are *logically dichotomous* (male and female, for example) rather than continuous. In personality type research using the Extraversion–Introversion dichotomy and gender, we would use the Phi coefficient if we are assuming that Extraversion and Introversion are logically polar opposites, that is, they are distinctly different, not differing amounts of the same thing.

Tetrachoric r is used when both variables are scored dichotomously, but when they also may be assumed to be *logically continuous*. In an experiment using pass-fail on an exam and the Extraversion–Introversion dichotomy, we would use Tetrachoric r if we assume people are distributed continuously from very Extraverted to very Introverted.

Phi and *Tetrachoric r* are good correlation coefficients to use in reliability studies when we are concerned with sensitivity to middle range scores. The product-moment correlation is greatly affected by extreme scores. For example, in table 2.5 (page 33) we calculated the correlation between height and weight. The greatest contribution to our product-moment correlation of .76 came from the two shortest and the two tallest children. Fortunately, the Phi coefficient and Tetrachoric r are not affected by extreme scores in the way product-moment correlation is. For example, several early MBTI internal consistency studies used Phi and Tetrachoric r. The fact that these correlations were similar in size to the product-moment correlations provided evidence that the MBTI assessment had the needed sensitivity near the mid-point.

3

Inferential Statistics

The measures we have covered thus far are called **descriptive statistics**. They accurately *describe* or summarize the characteristics of a set of measurements. However, we are often interested not only in describing some measurements but in making *inferences* from those measurements to people in general or to basic principles of behavior. In the example we used in the previous chapter, looking at the height and weight of 10 eight-year-olds, we were not interested so much in the relationship between height and weight in this sample of 10 children as we were in the relationship between height and weight in the population of all eight-year-old children, or at least in a larger group of eight-year-old children, perhaps all the eight-year-olds in a country or state.

To make inferences from a sample to a population requires some additional statistics—**inferential statistics**, sometimes also called *statistics of inference* or *sampling statistics*. Inferential statistics are methods used to generalize, or make inferences, from samples to populations by determining the probability that the results in a sample could have happened by chance alone.

In this chapter we will consider sampling, including a brief introduction to kinds of samples and sampling error; statistical significance; and Type I and Type II errors.

Sampling

In science we usually cannot measure *all* cases of something we are interested in. Because there usually are too many people or animals or events to allow us to measure all the cases, and because many are unavailable to us, we choose a smaller group to measure.

Overview

In most studies, we are selecting a **sample** from the **population**, which includes all possible measurements. Characteristics of samples are called statistics, while characteristics of populations are called **parameters.**

Random samples, also called *probability samples*, are critical when the results are to be applied directly, as in a poll to predict an election. Simple random sampling, stratified random sampling, and systematic random sampling are examples of random samples.

Most behavioral research tests theories and explores general principles, and findings will be combined with a variety of other studies. Because of this, it is common to use nonrandom methods, or *nonprobability samples*. Samples of convenience in which the researcher chooses readily available participants are typical. Self-selected samples, haphazard samples, and nonprobability systematic samples are examples of other nonrandom methods of selection. While easiest and least expensive, there is no way to judge the representativeness of these nonprobability samples.

Even when a sample is chosen well, there is still **sampling error** because the measurements came from a sample rather than from the whole population. No sample can perfectly reflect the population because of the peculiarities of the individuals chosen. All statistics have error because they differ somewhat from the parameters we'd get if we measured the whole population. When a sample is small, the sampling error tends to be large. As sample size increases in proportion to the population, the error decreases.

In most studies we cannot measure all cases, so we select a **sample** from the **population** of all possible participants. The population is the large group of interest, while the sample is the group we draw together to study. Characteristics of samples are called **statistics**, while characteristics of populations are called **parameters**. Because we typically cannot measure the whole population, we use statistics to estimate parameters. Technically the mean of a sample is a statistic (X), while the corresponding mean, μ, (the Greek *mu*) in the population is a parameter. Population values are typically represented by Greek letters, such as *sigma* (σ) for the population standard deviation, in contrast to the statistic SD based on a sample.

Kinds of Sampling

There are a variety of types of samples used in behavioral research. Samples can be either *probability samples*, using a random selection process, or *nonprobability samples*, chosen without random selection. We will look briefly at three kinds of random samples: simple random sampling, stratified random sampling, and systematic random sampling.

Probability Samples

In simple *random sampling*, which is really not very simple, every member of the population has an equal and independent chance of being included in the sample. For example, we could put the name of every person in the population on a slip of paper, put the slips in a container, and then have a blindfolded assistant pull out the number of slips we need for the sample. Simple random samples are fairly rare because it is typically not possible to identify *every* member of the population.

In *stratified random sampling*, the population is divided into subgroups, or strata, based on variables of importance in the study. After the population is divided into strata, a random sample is taken from each of the subgroups. The samples used for public opinion polls use this method. Because a simple random sample might by chance not include the correct proportions of factors that have been found relevant (urban vs. rural, male vs. female, age, education, etc.), the stratified random sampling process tries to assure that the sample is representative in these ways. While this approach works fairly well for pollsters, in most behavioral research we don't know what the relevant biasing factors are, or we have no way to control them, so this kind of sampling is not common.

Systematic random sampling involves selecting every kth element of the population, such as every seventh or twentieth individual. (The letter k commonly

Learning Key

Descriptive statistics: Describe or summarize data, without any implication of generalizability.

Inferential or Sampling statistics: Determine the likelihood that descriptive statistics found in a sample could have happened by chance alone.

represents the interval size). For this to be a truly random process, one must be able to assume the listing of the population is complete (no small feat!) and is random with respect to the variable of interest.

Nonprobability Samples

In nonprobability sampling, the sample is chosen by nonrandom methods. Typically nonprobability samples are chosen because they are more convenient and allow us to use participants who are available and are willing to volunteer.

The most common form of nonprobability sample is a *sample of convenience*, sometimes called an *accidental sample* or *sample of opportunity*. The researcher merely chooses readily available participants for the study. Students in an introductory psychology class are a familiar example of a convenience sample.

Self-selected samples, with open invitations to listeners or readers to respond; *haphazard samples,* recruited in public places where people have time on their hands; and *nonprobability systematic samples,* using a systematic but nonrandom process, are examples of other nonrandom methods of selection. Nonrandom sampling is least expensive in terms of time and money, but there is no way to judge how representative the sample is, especially with these last three types.

Types of samples are described in more detail in chapter 8. However, as you can see from this partial description, there are lots of different sampling methods and none of them are perfect. Despite what many people think, most samples in behavioral research are not random, but that is not a big problem. Random samples are critical when we want to apply findings directly, such as in conducting a poll to predict the outcome of an election. However, most behavioral research is not designed to be applied directly, but rather to test theories and explore general principles. Behavioral research findings will not stand on their own but will be combined with other studies using a variety of methods and participants to see what principles and theories are supported. If results from different studies point in the same direction, then we have convergence or converging evidence, as we will note again in chapter 8.

Sampling Error

Even when we have done our best to obtain a representative sample, we are still left with **sampling error**. We have measurements from only a sample rather than from the entire population. The chance differences in the selection of individuals from the population for our sample create the sampling error.

Each of the statistics we've described thus far—the mean, median, SD, and correlation coefficient—has some error, because the *statistics* we get with a sample differ somewhat from the values we'd get if we had the true measure of the whole population, the *parameters*. Mathematicians and statisticians have worked out formulas for estimating sampling errors. By using these formulas, we learn how much various samples might be expected to differ from one another simply by chance.

When our sample is small, the error tends to be relatively large. For example, if you were taking a multiple-choice exam at the end of a course, the sampling error regarding your understanding of the course content would be much greater if the test included only 3 items than if it included 50 items. That is, the chances are much greater you wouldn't get a good grade with a 3-item exam because the instructor might have asked about something you didn't understand and, if so, you could lose *one-third* of the points. With a 50-item exam, your score is more likely to reflect how much you understand. Not knowing a particular piece of content would only cost you 1/50th of the points. So, as the sample size increases in proportion to the population, the error decreases. As a rough general rule, the sampling error is inversely proportional to the square root of the number of measurements. Thus the error of sampling 10 cases is about ten times as large as the error of sampling 1,000 cases.

If there is a clearly biasing factor in our selection procedure, increasing the sample size may not help. If we are interested in sampling public opinion about attitudes on a social policy issue, but our selection procedure systematically and significantly over-includes or under-includes people with a particular position on the issue, it won't make much difference if we sample 100 people or 10,000. The results will be biased. However, if we don't have clearly biasing factors in our sampling, choosing a larger sample should help reduce sampling error.

It is important to keep in mind that *any measure we use has error*. If we select several samples from the same population and calculate the mean and SD of each sample, each mean and SD would have a slightly different value based on differences in the samples we select, as well as errors that arise in the measurement

Learning Key

Sample: Group selected for study. Measures describing a sample, like means and SDs, are called **statistics.**

Population: The larger group from which a sample is drawn. Measures describing the whole population, which we usually can only estimate, are called **parameters.** Statistics are used to estimate parameters.

Sampling error: Chance differences between sample statistics and population parameters, because the sample does not perfectly represent the population.

process. We will consider some of these other sources of error when we discuss reliability in chapter 4. Because of the fact that we have both sampling error as well as other kinds of error, *it is usually best to be cautious about putting much trust in small differences.*

Significance

Whenever different groups are compared, we will almost always find some differences and some relationships. However, differences and relationships can happen just by chance. Before we can generalize from any finding, we need to know if what was found was greater than what chance alone could account for.

Overview

Tests of **statistical significance** address the question: what is the probability that the finding could have happened by chance?

A variety of **tests of significance** are available to help determine the probability that a particular result occurred by chance alone. Among the most common are the **t-test**, used to compare the means of two groups, or to determine if a correlation is greater than zero; the **analysis of variance (ANOVA)**, used when comparing means of more than two groups; and **chi-square**, used when our data are frequencies.

The common convention in the behavioral sciences is that a .05 level of significance is the minimum standard. If results would have occurred by chance less than 5 times in 100, the results are called significant or fairly unlikely to have happened by chance alone. This level of significance is also indicated as p < .05 or .05 **alpha level**. A stricter or higher criterion of significance is p < .01, or probability is less than 1 in 100 that the results would have occurred only by chance. If the probability turns out to be less than .001 or .0001, that will be stated. The minimum acceptable level of significance must be stated before research begins.

In test manuals and research articles, significance is typically indicated by one or more asterisks: The symbol * typically means significance at the .05 level, ** means significance at the .01 level, while *** indicates significance at the .001 level.

When the probability of a result being due to chance is greater than 5 in 100 (p > .05), the finding is determined to be *not significant.* If p > .05, it is best not to interpret the result or claim a trend. If researchers believe more than chance is going on, they may try to refine the experimental technique or use a larger sample and try again to attain significance.

Tests of significance test the **null hypothesis (H_0)** that there are no differences other than chance. Researchers hope that the null hypothesis can be rejected, supporting the **research (or alternative) hypothesis**. When the research hypothesis is directional—predicting one group will score higher than the other—a **one-tailed test** can be used. Typically, however, **two-tailed tests** are used, either because there is no basis for predicting which group will score higher, or because the researcher wants to be able to interpret the results even if they come out differently than expected.

Many tests of significance require knowing the **degrees of freedom** (d.f.). Degrees of freedom are the number of values that are free to vary. Most commonly, the number of d.f. in a particular situation is one less than the number in the sample (N). Degrees of freedom is used instead of N in many statistical formulas because it has been found that statistics do a better job of estimating the corresponding parameter in the population when that is done.

Statistically significant does not mean **practically significant** or that a finding has importance. The larger a sample, the greater the likelihood that even a very small difference in means or correlations will be statistically significant. Thus, in large samples small but significant results must be interpreted carefully. Minimal differences can turn out to be statistically significant in large samples, yet not be very meaningful or important. Measures of *effect size* essentially are measures of practical significance. Together with common sense, they help us decide whether a statistically significant difference is big enough to be meaningful and useful information.

How do we know if the descriptive statistics we obtain from a sample could have happened just by chance? For this, we need to understand statistical decisions and the concept of statistical significance, the idea that a result appears to be more than chance alone could account for.

If we measure and compare two groups, we will almost always find some difference between their means. If we are correlating two variables in a study, we will almost always get at least a small relationship or correlation. We ask the following: When is a difference between two means greater than we would expect by chance alone? When is a correlation enough larger than zero to be more than just a chance finding? These questions are always answered in terms of probabilities. *There are no absolute certainties in statistics.* We are asking *what the odds* are that this is a chance finding.

Suppose we flip a coin 10 times and get 10 heads. We may wonder if this result can be expected by chance or whether our coin is biased. From tables of probability, we know that 10 heads on 10 flips can be expected once every 1,024 times, and 20 heads in 20 flips once in about a million times. While it may be very unlikely, if we flip coins several million times we can expect a sequence of 20 straight heads to occur some time by chance. So remarkable things can happen by chance alone. Some people win the lottery, even though the odds of a single ticket winning are extremely small.

In evaluating a particular research finding we are asking what the probability is that what was found could have happened by chance. A variety of **significance tests** or formulas are available to help us determine how likely it is that some particular result could have occurred by chance alone. Following are some of the common significance tests:

- The **t-test**, used when we want to compare the means of two groups, illustrated later in this chapter. The t-test also is used when we want to determine if a correlation is greater than zero, illustrated in appendix B.

- **Analysis of variance (ANOVA),** used when we are comparing means of more than two groups, explained in appendix B.

- **Chi-square**, used in tables of frequencies, comparing obtained frequencies with frequencies expected in each cell of the table based on row and column totals, as demonstrated in appendix B.

From the results of computations using a test of significance, and reference to readily available statistical tables, we can determine the probability—the odds—of our particular results occurring by chance. We're used to hearing odds

---

Learning Key

Statistical significance: The probability that a result happened by chance alone is so low (for example, less than 5 times in 100) that we conclude the result can be generalized. Significance does not mean importance.

Tests of significance: Formulas using statistics from sample results to determine how likely those results could have happened by chance alone. Most common ones are: the **t-test**, used when means of two groups are compared; **Analysis of Variance or ANOVA**, used when means of three or more groups are compared; and **chi-square**, used when the data are frequencies.

Practical significance: Results are meaningful in some useful way (what you thought significance meant before you learned about statistics!)

Alpha level: Level of significance chosen, such as $p < .05$ or $p < .01$.

expressed as probabilities when we hear a weather forecast. If the weather fore-caster says there is a 10% chance of rain, we know there is a chance we will get rained on, but we also know there is a much greater chance it will not rain; we know that while it could rain, the odds are sufficiently low that we can go ahead with our outdoor plans, maybe sticking in an umbrella just in case. When we do a test of significance, we are doing something similar when we state up front what odds we are willing to accept that the results are merely by chance.

Levels of Significance

By common convention in the behavioral sciences, 5% is the minimum standard of risk we are prepared to take. If our results would have occurred by chance less than 5 times in 100, we say our results are significant. When we say a result is **significant**, we are saying that it is fairly unlikely to have happened by chance alone. If this criterion is met, we can say our results are

- significant at the .05 (point "oh" five) level,
- $p < .05$ (probability less than .05),
- p-value less than .05, or
- significant at a .05 **alpha level.**

Each of those phrases means the same thing: Our results would have hap-pened *by chance alone* less that 5 times in 100.

While the .05 level of significance is the minimum accepted in the behav-ioral sciences, there is a stricter criterion of significance, $p < .01$, or the probability that the chance occurrence is less than 1 time in 100. Because the results are less likely to be due to chance, we say the .01 level is a *higher level* (or stricter level) of significance. Researchers typically insist on significance at least at the .05 level, but prefer the .01 level. If the probability turns out to be less than .001 or .0001, that will be stated, but most researchers in the behavioral sciences will be happy to settle for significance at the .05 or .01 level, and whatever level they will settle for is stated up front, before the research begins. We'll consider a bit later the problem of Type I and Type II errors, which are greatly affected by our choice of .05 or .01.

The .05 level of significance is the generally accepted minimum in the behavioral sciences because of the difficulties involved in getting greater precision when dealing with the vagaries of human behavior. If we were building bridges and testing the strength of the steel beams used in construction, we certainly would want a higher level of significance. We aren't prepared to have a bridge collapse every twentieth time we cross it! In conducting tests on safety of potable water, the standard may be .0000001, or less than one time in 10 million that the results are due to chance. Minimum levels of significance vary from one branch of science to another, depending on the levels of precision that are possible and required.

Indicating Significance

In test manuals and research articles, the significance of a finding is typically indicated by one or more asterisks.

One asterisk (*) typically means significance at the .05 level.

Two asterisks (**) show significance at the .01 level.

Three asterisks (***) indicate significance at the .001 level.

We might read in a table that for the difference between two means, the value of t was 2.92*. We would know that the t-test comparing the means was significant at the .05 level. You can think of this use of asterisks as analogous to hotel or restaurant ratings: the more stars the better. One star may be OK, but we may prefer two or three. Usually the footnotes in a research table will indicate the meaning of the symbols used in the table. We will see where the 2.92 in this example comes from in the following illustration of how significance works.

If a statistical test shows that the probability of a result being due to chance is greater than (>) 5 in 100 (p > .05), we would need to conclude that the finding is a chance one, or that we don't have enough evidence to say it is not chance. We would state that the finding is *not significant*, or we could simply indicate p > .05. If we still believe there is something more than chance going on, we may try to refine our experimental technique, or use a larger sample and try again to see if we can attain a finding of significance.

How Significance Works: An Illustration

To see how significance works, and to demonstrate that there is nothing magic about significance tests, let's design an experiment and follow the process of using a significance test, the t-test, to compare two means.

Let's suppose that on the basis of some things we've observed, we believe Extraverts (Es) and Introverts (Is) differ on a psychological characteristic, and that we have located a valid test, the XYZ Inventory, which measures this characteris-

---

Learning Key

Null hypothesis: Tentative assumption that there are no differences in data except chance factors. Every inferential statistic is testing this hypothesis, which we will be able to reject if the results are significant.

Research (or alternative) hypothesis: The research idea that gains support if we find statistical significance and are able to reject the null hypothesis.

Degrees of freedom: Number of values free to vary, usually N - 1; necessary for determining critical value for a significance test.

tic. We set out to see whether Es and Is differ on this characteristic, using under-graduate psychology students available at a nearby university as our participants.

Before we can begin our experiment, we have to make some decisions.

- What will our hypotheses be?
- Which significance test will we use?
- Will we use a one- or two-tailed test?
- What will be our minimum level of significance?
- How many degrees of freedom will we have?

What will our hypotheses be?

The first thing we must do as we design our experiment is state our hypothesis, that is, the idea we are testing in our experiment and what we expect to find. Our **research hypothesis** will be that Es and Is differ on XYZ Inventory scores. How-ever, we need another hypothesis as well. As good scientists using a significance test, we will also state the null hypothesis, often abbreviated H_0, which assumes there are no differences except chance factors. Our **null hypothesis** is that there is no real difference between Es and Is on XYZ Inventory scores. We will hope to be able to reject the null hypothesis by finding that the differences we obtain will be significant or greater than chance alone could account for. All tests of significance are based on this idea that any differences we find are chance ones.

If the test of significance says the results are likely to have happened by chance, we will conclude that the null hypothesis is supported. Of course, since we think there is a real difference, we will hope to have support for the research hypothesis, which is also called the **alternative hypothesis** because it is alternative to the null hypothesis of no difference. We will hope that the null hypothesis turns out to be very unlikely to be true, so that we can *reject* the null hypothesis.

Which significance test will we use?

Because we have means for two groups (Es and Is) to compare, and XYZ Inven-tory scores are reasonably normal and scores are on an interval scale, the t-test is the appropriate test of significance for our use in this experiment. The t-statistic that we will use in the t-test has some similarities to the z-score you learned about earlier, but rather than having a single distribution (the normal curve) like the z-score, t has a whole family of distributions, or different shapes, which vary as a function of the sample size. We will need to be aware of this when we get to the question concerning degrees of freedom. Incidentally, there is no relationship between the t-statistic that is used in the t-test described here and the standard score called a T-score, described on page 26; fortunately, one is typically capitalized and the other is not.

Will we use a one- or two-tailed test?

Research hypotheses can be either directional or nondirectional. They are directional when our research prediction is that one group will score higher than the other, and they are nondirectional when either (a) we don't know who will come out on top, or (b) we want to know if we have significance whichever way the results come out. If we have a directional hypothesis (we are predicting one way the results will come out), we can use a one-tailed test, which will give us a higher chance of getting significance than if we used a two-tailed test. However, if we use a one-tailed test, we sacrifice the possibility of interpreting results that come out in the opposite direction from what we expected. For that reason, researchers typically use two-tailed tests. For those who are curious, the difference between one- and two-tailed tests is explored further in appendix D, One-Tailed and Two-Tailed Tests, on page 197.

But, getting back to Es and Is and the XYZ Inventory: We will take the more conservative approach and use a two-tailed test, even though we suspect that Es will get higher scores on the XYZ Inventory. Our null hypothesis is that Es and Is will not differ on XYZ Inventory scores. Our research hypothesis is that Es and Is do differ on XYZ scores.

What will be our minimum level of significance?

We will set .05 as our desired level of significance or alpha (α) level. This minimal level of significance is appropriate in this case because of the exploratory nature of the study and our use of a fairly small sample of 20 students, 10 Es and 10 Is.

How many degrees of freedom will we have?

The t-statistic has a family of distributions varying as a function of degrees of freedom. So what are degrees of freedom? **Degrees of freedom** refers to the number of values (or scores) which are free to vary. We use degrees of freedom, commonly abbreviated d.f., in looking up the critical value of a statistic to see if the results we found are significant.

Most commonly, the number of d.f. in a particular situation is one less than the number in the sample (N). For example, suppose we have four scores (N) and know that they add up to 35. Three of those scores could take on any value—we have the freedom to set them at any number we like—while the fourth would be fixed. To illustrate, if the three scores were 5, 10, and 15, the fourth score would have to be 5 for the sum to equal 35. The number of degrees of freedom in this case is N (4) minus 1, or 3.

$$\text{d.f.} = N - 1 \qquad = 4 - 1 = 3$$

For a more everyday example, imagine you are baking a cake and the directions say to use a 13 x 9 x 2 inch pan. You go to your cupboard and find a variety of pans, but not that size. What can you do? Multiplying 13 times 9 times 2 tells you that you need a pan with 234 cubic inches. Each of our pans has three dimensions, length, width, and depth, so our N is 3. If we know two of our dimensions, the other one is fixed if all the batter is to fit in. We can choose a 10 x 9 pan, but we have lost a degree of freedom in that now our pan must be at least 2.6 inches deep.

Similarly, when we calculate a mean of a group of 10 scores, such as our 10 E scores on the XYZ Inventory, we find the mean is a particular value, and this puts a restriction on our data. While 9 of the scores could move around, the tenth score would be fixed so that the mean would still be the number we calculated. For any sample on which we have only one restriction (limitation), the number of d.f. will be N - 1.

Determining the degrees of freedom is a part of the process of performing most tests of significance. In addition, the degrees of freedom is used instead of N in many statistical formulas because it has been found that statistics do a better job of estimating the corresponding parameter in the population when that is done. For example, as we noted in chapter 2, most standard deviation formulas use N -1 instead of N.

The experiment

We have determined the following in our design of the statistical information we need to consider before we begin our experiment.

- We have stated our hypotheses, both the null hypothesis and the research, or alternative, hypothesis.
- We have chosen the statistical test we will use, the t-test.
- We have determined that we will use a two-tailed test.
- Our minimum level of significance will be .05.
- The degrees of freedom is N - 1.

We give the XYZ Inventory to 10 students that we know are Extraverts and to 10 that we know are Introverts. We get the following results:

Es (Group 1): Mean = 64.52   SD = 12.32
Is (Group 2): Mean = 46.27   SD = 14.11

Next we will look at the process for determining whether we have significant results in this study. Please note this illustration is only to help you understand how tests of significance work, not to teach you to do such calculations yourself.

Determining t

Our formula for t shows we will subtract one mean from the other and divide by the standard error of the difference. To determine t, we must find the standard error of the difference (S_{diff}), and for that we will need to find the standard error of the mean (S_M) for each of our groups.

$$t = \frac{Mean_1 - Mean_2}{S_{diff}}$$

Standard Error of the Mean. The standard error of the mean (S_M) is an estimate of the standard deviation of a distribution of means. To understand S_M, let's just imagine we know for a fact that the mean XYZ Inventory score of all the Extraverted college students in the world is 65. Suppose we take a random sample of 50 college students and compute the sample mean XYZ score. If we repeated our experiment many times, taking different random samples of 50 college students, we'd get different results each time because of sampling error. That is, chance factors would cause us to get a sample of people each time with somewhat higher or lower XYZ scores than the true mean score of the whole population.

The sample means for the Es on the XYZ Inventory for all these experiments would themselves form a distribution. The mean of this distribution of means should be about the same as our population mean of 65, but the standard deviation of this distribution of means would be smaller than the standard deviations of the original groups because each mean would have canceled out some of the variability. For each sample, we have just one middle number rather than all the individual numbers, with the highs and lows canceling each other, so to speak. The standard error of the mean is our estimate of what the standard deviation of this distribution of means would be.

The S_M equals the standard deviation of the raw scores divided by the square root of the degrees of freedom (the sample size minus 1).

$$S_M = \frac{SD}{\sqrt{N-1}}$$

Group 1 (Es)
S_M = 12.32 ÷ the square root of 9 (3) = 4.11

Group 2 (Is)
S_M = 14.11 ÷ the square root of 9 (3) = 4.70

Standard Error of the Difference. For the next step in determining t, we compute the standard error of the difference (S_{diff}), which is an estimate of the standard deviation of a distribution of differences between the means of two groups. Imagine again that we do our experiment many times. Just as mean XYZ scores for Es and for Is will vary some from experiment to experiment, the amount of difference between the E mean and the I mean will vary from experiment to experiment, and these differences would themselves form a distribution.

The standard error of the difference is an estimate of the standard deviation of this distribution of differences between the means. Mathematically, it can be shown that the standard error of the difference is determined by the size of the standard errors of the mean of each of the groups. The S_{diff} is found by squaring the standard error of the mean for each group, adding them together, and taking the square root of the sum, or

$$S_{diff} = \sqrt{S_{M_1}{}^2 + S_{M_2}{}^2}$$

S_{diff} = the square root of (4.112 + 4.702) = 6.24.

Calculating t. Next we are ready to calculate t by dividing the difference between the two means by the S_{diff}.

$$t = \frac{Mean_1 - Mean_2}{S_{diff}} = \frac{64.52 - 46.27}{6.24} = 2.92$$

We turn to a table of the t-distribution in a statistics book to find that the critical value of t for

- 9 degrees of freedom (N - 1; 10 subjects in each group minus 1)

- alpha = .05

- a two-tailed test.

The answer we find is 2.262. Any t value we calculate equal to, or greater than, this critical value will be significant at the .05 level. Therefore, our t of 2.92 is significant.

What is a critical value? When we do a significance test and want to know if the value of t (or F or chi-square) that we have calculated is significant, we use tables that statisticians have prepared, which are widely available in statistics books or from other sources. In these tables, for every combination of significance level and number of degrees of freedom, a number—a critical value—is listed. This critical value is the lowest number the statistic can have and still be significant at that level for that number of degrees of freedom.

To determine t, we

- stated our hypotheses, chose our statistical test, determined it would be a two-tailed test, set a minimum significance level at .05, and determined our d.f. to be N - 1;

- calculated the standard error of the mean (S_M) for each group;
- computed the standard error of the difference (S_{diff});
- divided the difference between the two means by the S_{diff};
- looked in a table of the t-distribution to find the critical value of the t for data with our statistical information; and
- compared our calculation of t with the critical value we found in the t-distribution.

Note particularly that to get this result, no magical incantations were chanted. No mysterious processes occurred. What we used were simply descriptive statistics of our groups (N, mean, SD) with formulas that used squaring, adding and subtracting, multiplying and dividing, and square-root taking. We then referred to a table that statisticians have shown, and mathematically proven, accurately reflects how much difference we could get by chance. You may never need to calculate a t-test yourself, but you will at least know how the basic process works.

As a way to wrap up our consideration of the t-test for mean differences, let's take a visual look at what we have done. Figure 3.1 graphically displays the distribution of scores of Es and Is on the XYZ Inventory that we would predict based on our samples, using the means and SDs we found. These distributions of Es and Is are shown with solid lines.

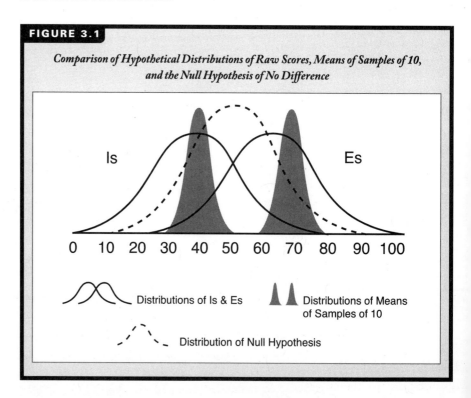

FIGURE 3.1

Comparison of Hypothetical Distributions of Raw Scores, Means of Samples of 10, and the Null Hypothesis of No Difference

Is   Es

0   10   20   30   40   50   60   70   80   90   100

Distributions of Is & Es   Distributions of Means of Samples of 10

Distribution of Null Hypothesis

If we did our experiment many times, we would expect *means* of samples of 10 Extraverts and 10 Introverts to fall in the narrow solid black distributions. The *standard deviations* of these narrow solid black distributions are the standard errors of the mean we computed. The null hypothesis we are testing in our significance test is displayed with a dotted line. Our null hypothesis is that there are no differences in XYZ scores between Es and Is—that our E and I samples are really just random samples from a single population of persons responding to the XYZ Inventory, a population in which E–I makes no difference.

We've illustrated how statistical significance is determined through an example of a study using the t-test for mean differences. Appendix B has illustrations for the t-test to determine if a correlation coefficient is significant, as well as the analysis of variance (ANOVA) for mean differences with more than two groups, and chi-square for differences in frequency.

Statistical Significance and Practical Significance

Now that we have found a significant result, it is important to note: *Statistically significant and **practically significant** are not the same thing*. Significance in statistics has to do with the likelihood that our result is a chance phenomenon, not whether it is important. We noted earlier the significant correlation between ice cream sales and number of homicides in New York City, related no doubt to higher ice cream sales and murder rates in warm weather. This finding is not meaningful or useful in a practical way. Closing down ice cream stores would not save lives. However, it is still *statistically* significant because the finding is not a chance one. It's just not useful or important information.

If our sample is too small, it may be hard to get significant results. It can be shown mathematically, and may be apparent to you as you look at the formulas given above, that the larger the sample size, the larger the t value we will find, given a particular mean difference. Therefore, the likelihood is greater that our experiment will have significant results. This principle of the larger the sample size, the greater the likelihood of significance will be true with any significance test. The principle about sample size and significance helps us know that if we fail to get significance in one sample, we may want to repeat an experiment, but with a larger N the next time.

On the other hand, large sample size is often a reason that a statistically significant result is not also practically significant. A small difference found in a large sample is less likely to have occurred by chance than the same size small difference found in a small sample, so significance is more likely to be found with the large sample, even for a very small actual difference. Thus we may get statistical significance when the differences are in fact inconsequential. We also want to avoid very large samples because of the costs involved in using that many participants.

Suppose a political poll using a very large sample shows a statistically significant difference in opinions of Democrats versus Republicans on some issue The poll finds 74% of Democrats and 75% of Republicans support the issue. Even though the difference may be statistically significant, nearly the same proportion of both parties support the issue; the statistical difference is not a meaningful difference. Or, suppose we gave a test with 250 possible points to very large groups of Extraverts and Introverts. A small two point difference between Es and Is might be statistically significant, but in relation to the 250 point scale it might not be very important or meaningful. It is *not* a chance finding, but it may not be practically significant.

Measures of *effect size* essentially are measures of practical significance. It is one thing to know something didn't happen by chance, but how much effect did one variable have on the other? Is the difference between the variables large enough to give us useful information?

Effect size helps with the problem of sample size by showing the actual size of a significant difference, irrespective of the size of the sample. There are a variety of measures of effect size. We will note here two of the most common.

We met one measure of effect size already in the last chapter. We got the *coefficient of determination*—what variance accounted for is called when used for effect size—by squaring a correlation coefficient. A correlation coefficient isn't in numbers that have meaning in ordinary terms, but squaring the correlation tells us in percentage terms how big a relationship exists between the variables. Once we know the percentage of the effect that the variables have on each other, then we have information for deciding whether the effect of a significant correlation is big enough to be meaningful in some useful way.

Another effect-size measure is called *Cohen's d*. It is one we can use when we have compared the means of two groups and found a significant t-test. Cohen's d takes the actual difference between the two means and divides it by either the standard deviation of the dependent measure or the pooled standard deviation of both variables. The pooled standard deviation is found by taking the square root of $[(SD_1^2 + SD_2^2) / 2]$. You don't need to know the formula. All you really need to know is that usually a d of 0.2 is seen as indicating a small effect, 0.5 is seen as indicating a medium effect, and 0.8 or larger indicates a large effect. If we read an article and a Cohen's d of less than 0.2 is reported, we can probably conclude the effect is minimal, even if the result was significant. The larger the value, the more we can conclude the effect is likely to be practically significant as well as statistically significant.

For example, our illustration earlier in this chapter about differences between Extraverts and Introverts on XYZ test scores found statistical significance at the .05 level. We had a mean score of 64.52 for Extraverts, and a mean score of 46.27

for Introverts, giving us a point difference on the XYZ Test of 18.25. Our standard deviations were 12.32 for Extraverts and 14.11 for Introverts. Using the formula in the previous paragraph, we find a pooled standard deviation of 13.25. Dividing the 18.25 XYZ point difference between the mean scores of Extraverts and Introverts by the pooled standard deviation of 13.25 results in a *Cohen's d of 1.38*. The difference we found is not only statistically significant but represents a large, practically significant effect as well, because our Cohen's d exceeds the 0.8 definition of a large effect by a wide margin. How we will use this finding depends on the nature of the characteristic the XYZ test measured, the options we have available, and how this fits with other research.

Because statistical significance depends so much on the size of the sample, some journals now require authors to provide a measure of effect size whenever they report a test of significance. Measures of effect size help us determine whether results that are statistically significant are also practically significant. However, be aware that practical significance is also a matter of common sense. Whether a statistically significant difference is big enough to make a difference depends on the situation, and upon what the research community has agreed is important. The same thing can be important in one situation and not in another. For example, if I need a new part for my lawnmower, I want the part to fit reasonably well so my lawnmower runs. However, if that part were to be part of the space shuttle instead, the tolerances for accuracy of fit would be much smaller. So, we want to know that a particular research finding is significant—that it is not likely to be a chance finding—but deciding whether the finding will be useful is a somewhat subjective process.

Type I and Type II Errors

Each time we do an experiment, we can have one of two kinds of errors, and for each experiment we must decide which error would have the greater cost.

Overview

When a test of significance is used, two kinds of errors can occur. A **Type I error** occurs if the null hypothesis is rejected when it is true, that is, finding a significant result in the sample when there is no such difference in the population. A **Type II error** occurs if we fail to reject the null hypothesis when it is false—if significance is not found in the sample, when in reality there is a difference in the population.

A Type I error is likely to occur 5% of the time when the significance level is .05. There is no simple way to know how often Type II errors happen. To keep Type I errors to a minimum, statistical tests are planned before experiments begin. Efforts to reduce Type I errors tend to increase Type II errors, and reducing Type II errors tends to increase Type I errors. Researchers must decide which risks are greatest when carrying out an experiment, knowing there is a trade-off.

When we use a test of significance, we are trying to determine how likely it is that our experimental results happened by chance. While we can learn what the odds are, we don't know the reality—what exists in the whole population. One of two kinds of errors can occur each time we do an experiment.

- A **Type I error** occurs if we reject the null hypothesis (H_0) when it is true.

- A **Type II error** occurs if we fail to reject the null hypothesis (H_0) when it is false.

A Type I error means we say the results are significant when *really* they are due to chance. For example, our significant t-test finding led us to believe that Es and Is differ on the characteristic measured by the XYZ Inventory, but perhaps in the whole population there is no difference between Es and Is, and what we got was just a chance finding, perhaps because of some peculiarities of the sample we chose for the experiment. A Type I error is likely to occur 5% of the time when our significance level is .05.

A Type II error means that we say our results are *not* significant when there actually is a difference. This is not just a chance finding. For example, suppose the t for our experiment had not been big enough to yield significance and we had to conclude there is no difference between Es and Is on XYZ, when in reality, in the whole population of college students, there is such a difference, just as we had suspected. The fact we did not find significance would be a Type II error. While the alpha level tells us how often Type I errors are likely to occur, we have no way to know how often Type II errors happen; we just know that they do. For this reason, we hope researchers don't give up on good ideas that did not lead to significance the first time and will try again, perhaps with improved procedures or larger samples.

Figure 3.2 shows the relationship of Type I and Type II errors to the decision we make, based on our significance test, and the true status of the null hypothesis in the population we are estimating with our sample.

FIGURE 3.2

	Null Hypothesis (H_0) is really	
Decision	True	False
Accept H_0	ok	Type II error
Reject H_0	Type I error	ok

Type I and Type II errors are not limited to experiments, but occur in many aspects of life. Suppose a pharmaceutical developer submits a new drug to the Food and Drug Administration (FDA) for approval. The FDA can make either error. The FDA can approve the drug, which eventually turns out to have unanticipated dangerous side effects (Type II error), or the FDA can commit a Type I error by disapproving, or holding up approval, of the drug which is perfectly safe and effective. Either error has its costs, but the political and legal realities lead the FDA generally to try hardest to avoid Type II errors.

On the international scene, suppose a government has intelligence that a potential enemy has new, very dangerous weapons. Which error is less costly? To incorrectly assume the enemy does not have such weapons and do nothing, or incorrectly assume the enemy has them and take unnecessary but costly military action against the presumed enemy? Intelligence is always less than perfect, and governments must decide where the greatest risk lies.

To keep Type I errors to a minimum in research, we plan which statistical test we will use *before* we begin our experiment. That way we are not tempted to choose a statistical test after the fact just because it yields significance for our results. It is OK to choose a statistical test in advance that fits how we think the results should turn out, however.

We need to expect Type I errors—getting significance by chance—5% of the time with a .05 level of significance when we look at research literature. For example, one study in the MBTI literature used a total of 104 significance tests in analysis of the results and found 23 significant differences in those 104 tests. One would expect to get 5.2 significant differences by chance alone from that many significance tests, using the $p < .05$ level of significance (104 x .05 = 5.2). We'll never know for sure if significant findings in a study such as that are due to chance or which ones are due to chance, of course. However, 14 of the

Learning Key

Type I error: Saying results are significant when really they are due to chance. The likelihood of a Type I error is the same as **alpha**, the significance level. At the .05 level, the probability of making a Type I error is 5%.

Type II error: Saying results are *not* significant when the differences are real; the differences really are *not* due to chance.

significant differences in this study were from the 26 significance tests involving the Extraversion–Introversion dichotomy, 6 were from the 26 involving Sensing–Intuition, 1 was from the 26 involving Thinking–Feeling, and 2 were from the 26 involving Judging–Perceiving. Because .05 x 26 is 1.3, we probably should disregard the differences attributed to the T–F and J–P dichotomies. They well could have been chance findings. There is no reason to fault the author for reporting these findings. This was the first major experimental study in an area of great interest to many MBTI users, and thus a fishing-expedition approach was quite appropriate. We just need to be careful how we interpret these findings, particularly until there is more research available on that topic.

Remember that when lots of significance tests are done, there will likely be some Type I errors. We will reject the null hypothesis when it is true, believing the result is significant when it really is just a chance difference. We can reduce the risk of a Type I error by using a smaller p-value, insisting on significance at the .01 level or higher, for instance.

While we don't want to make Type I errors, we also do not want to make Type II errors. If we set our significance level at .01, we have reduced the likelihood of a Type I error, but we have increased the likelihood of a Type II error. So we have a trade-off and must decide, given the risks involved, which error is most important to avoid. That will depend on the nature of the study and what is involved if we make a mistake. One can reduce Type II errors by lowering the level of significance and by having larger samples.

Choosing Significance Tests

Determination that a particular statistical test is the right one for a given situation is not an easy task. Each significance test has a variety of assumptions for its appropriate use.

Overview

Some statistical tests are more likely than others to yield a significant result in a given situation. They are said to be more *powerful*. Determination that a particular statistical test is the right one to use in a given situation often requires consulting specialists in statistics. In most reputable journals, an evaluation of the statistics that have been used is part of the process of determining whether a particular article should be published.

Most statistical tests assume that all observations are *independent*—one observation doesn't influence another. Many also assume we have *interval data* that is more or less *normally distributed*. When those assumptions are not met, we may need to use some different significance tests, called *nonparametric tests*. In addition, some tests are more *powerful* than others for a given situation. A powerful test is more likely to correctly reject a false null hypothesis and therefore yield a significant result, given the same data.

Specialists in statistics can determine which statistical test is the right one for a given situation and it is good to use these experts when we do research. While most graduate students are required to take some statistics training, I'm talking here about people who've had more than one or two courses.

The good news is that in most reputable journals, the editor includes an evaluation of the statistics that have been used as part of the process of determining whether a particular article should be published. Therefore, in a published article you won't ordinarily have to wonder whether the right statistical test was chosen.

Exercises and Questions to Check Your Understanding

1. **Here are some descriptions of some samples. Place in the blank the letter that best identifies the kind of sample described.**

   a. *simple random sample*

   b. *stratified random sample*

   c. *systematic random sample*

   d. *sample of convenience*

   _____ A. During development of Form M of the MBTI instrument, researchers gathered a sample—using random digit dialing—in which they tried to match proportions of people in the sample with proportions of people in the 1990 U.S. census based on factors such as age, gender, and ethnicity.

   _____ B. The director of nursing wants to know which of two training methods is most effective to prepare nurses in her hospital for the periodic re-certification exams they must take. Using a numbered list of names of the nurses in her hospital, she uses a table of random numbers to select two groups of nurses, one group to be trained with training method A and the other group to have training method B.

_____ C. To study the effectiveness of counseling in retention of students, the director of a university counseling center studied the records of students who made appointments for counseling at the center the previous year to see if there were differences in retention for students seen 0, 1-3, 4-6, or 7 or more sessions.

2. Mark the correct answer to finish this statement. Sampling error is

   A. Avoidable if correct sampling procedures are used

   B. Greater the larger the sample

   C. Greater the smaller the sample

   D. Unlikely if we have a truly random sample

3. Which is the higher level of significance? Circle the correct answer.

   A. $p < .01$

   B. $p < .05$

4. Suppose you read this statement: *The correlation between grade point average (GPA) and scores on the ABC achievement test was .69**.*

   What do the asterisks mean? _____

5. Suppose you read this statement: *For the difference between the means, t = 1.7 (p > .05).*

   A. Should you conclude that the researcher found statistical significance?

   _____

   B. What evidence do you find in the statement for your conclusion?

   _____

6. Suppose you read this statement: *The null hypothesis was rejected (p < .01).*

   A. Should you conclude that the researcher found statistical significance?

   _____

   B. What evidence do you find in the statement for your conclusion?

   _____

7. **For which of these studies would p < .05 be an acceptable minimum level of significance? Mark all that apply.**

   A. Testing the precision of a formula for a medical drug.

   B. Testing whether there are mean differences on an IQ test between 25 students who prefer Extraversion and 25 who prefer Introversion.

   C. Testing for differences between older and younger consumers in flavors of coffee they purchased.

   D. Testing for level of lead content in paint chips from 1,000 older houses.

8. **Mark the answer that correctly finishes this statement. *The larger the sample, all other things being equal,***

   A. the more likely the null hypothesis will be rejected.

   B. the less likely the null hypothesis will be rejected.

9. **Type I and Type II errors have to do with the concept of true and false. Mark these statements true or false.**

   _____A.   A Type I error means saying that results are significant when in reality the results are due to chance.

   _____ B.   The level of significance helps us know how likely it is that there is a Type I error.

   _____ C.   We can reduce Type I errors by using a lower level of significance.

   _____ D.   If we reject the null hypothesis when it is true, we have a Type II error.

   _____ E.   A Type II error is the same as the level of significance.

   _____ F.   Researchers can avoid Type I and Type II errors through careful research designs and procedures.

   _____ G.   Which error (Type I or Type II) is most important to avoid depends on the consequences in each particular situation.

2

Characteristics of Good Psychological Tests

If we want to measure how tall we are, we use a tape measure to see how far the top of our head is from the floor, and we make the measurement without much ado because we assume our tape measure is reasonably accurate. This attitude that measuring instruments can be trusted tends to carry over into things psychological. There are thousands of psychological tests. Many have little value, but others perform well. What are the characteristics of a good test? In part II we see that a good test is

- reliable,
- valid,
- has appropriate norms, and
- has good usability.

In chapter 4, we consider reliability, the consistency of a test. In chapter 5, we look at the evidence needed to establish validity, whether a test measures what it intends to measure. Norms and factors that make a test user-friendly are described in chapter 6.

4
Reliability

Tests of any kind, psychological or physical, must be used intelligently. They are invented to do a particular job. Some succeed and some don't. Tests are valuable when they satisfy certain requirements and are used for the purposes for which they were intended. One requirement is that a test should be reliable.

In this chapter, we will discuss reliability, which has to do with the degree of precision in a test that allows it to get consistent results. We will look at three kinds of reliability: test-retest, alternate form, and internal consistency. We will discuss the standard error of measurement. We will also look at item response theory, a newer method for looking at a test's precision.

What is Reliability?

A first consideration when evaluating a test or research instrument is determining if it is reliable. If you can't measure something twice with the same instrument and get about the same answer each time, the measurements are not worth very much. You want to be able to repeat the results.

Overview

Reliability refers to how consistently a test measures what it attempts to measure. Reliability is determined by correlating one set of scores with another set obtained from the same people and is expressed as a correlation coefficient ranging from .00 (no reliability) to 1.00 (perfect reliability).

Any measurement has two parts: *true score* and *error*. The true score is the actual amount of the measured characteristic that is present. Error is the amount above or below that figure which may be due to inadequacies of our measurement instruments or in our data collection procedures. The less error in our measurement, the more precise and consistent it will be. In other words, the less error, the more reliable our test will be.

Reliability refers to how consistently an instrument measures what it attempts to measure. With an intelligence test, we want to consistently come up with the same IQ each time a person is tested, assuming conditions have not changed. With an interest or aptitude test, we want to come up with the same pattern of interests or abilities. With a personality test, we want to come up with the same pattern or type if the person is tested again.

We use the correlation coefficient as the statistic for reporting the relative reliability or unreliability of a test. By correlating one set of scores with another set of scores from the same people, we get a measure of the test's reliability. Reliabilities are expressed as correlation coefficients which range from .00 (the absence of reliability) to 1.00 (perfect reliability).

Let's suppose we are gathering the heights of our 10 eight-year-olds and use an elastic ruler. Let's suppose further that we suspect the ruler might be giving us some unreliable results, so we check it out by measuring one of the children—the one that's 51 inches tall—ten times and get ten different answers, ranging from 50 to 53 inches. We can assume the child did not grow or shrink a few inches during the 15 minutes we are taking the measurements and that the true height is 51 inches the whole time. Therefore, something must be wrong with the ruler we are using. It is unreliable because it does not produce consistent findings with repeated measurements.

Now let's suppose we measure the heights again, using a steel tape measure. To compare the reliability of our instruments, we could measure our test child again ten times. Chances are we'd find some variability, though less than a quarter inch either way from the child's true height. The results would be much more consistent than with the elastic ruler.

One way to think about reliability is to think of any measurement as having two parts: *true score* and *error*. In our example, the true score was 51 inches; error is the amount we obtained above or below that figure. Error does not mean a mistake has been made. It is simply a recognition that there will always be some inaccuracies in measurement. We are talking here about *measurement error* related to the inadequacies of our measurement instruments, not sampling error which occurs any time we draw a sample, and which is related to the fact that our sample does not perfectly match the population from which it was drawn. Our interest is in finding out how much measurement error there is, and in reducing it if we can. If a measure is relatively free from error, we call it reliable. From test theory we know that the true score is the average of the scores we would get if we did the measurement an unlimited number of times under the same conditions. Of course, we can't measure anything an infinite number of times, so we must estimate the true score from the score we actually found. Error is assumed to be random and uncorrelated with the true score, that is, it can raise a score as often as it lowers the score. It has been found that, in the long run, the mean of the error will equal zero, and the mean of the scores we obtain will equal the mean of the true scores. In other words, even with our unreliable elastic ruler we can expect that the measurements would average out to the true heights of the children if we measured them many, many times, and if we assumed this special elastic contracted as well as expanded. Obviously, because we typically make a measurement only once, we want to use an instrument that has little error so that our obtained score is pretty close to the true score. We want our measuring instrument to be reliable.

Kinds of Reliability

There are three common ways of determining reliability: test-retest reliability, alternate form reliability, and internal consistency reliability. Internal consistency reliability has two common subtypes: split-half reliability and coefficient alpha.

Overview

Test-retest reliability measures stability of test scores over time by administering the same test to the same people on two different occasions. It is appropriately used when the measured characteristic remains fairly stable over time, like intelligence, ability, or personality. Typically, the shorter the interval between administrations, the higher the correlation. No test has perfect test-retest reliability.

Alternate form reliability is similar to test-retest reliability except that another equivalent form of the test, with different items, is administered the second time. The difficulty of creating two good tests and the possibility that the two forms will not be exactly equivalent makes this type of reliability rare.

Internal consistency reliability examines the degree of consistency across items rather than stability over time. It asks if all items are measuring the same thing. The test only needs to be administered once. Two forms of internal consistency reliability are **split-half reliability** and coefficient alpha. Split-half reliability is produced by dividing a single scale into two halves. Scores from items in one half of a scale are correlated with scores from the other half of the scale. A variety of methods are used to split the items into two halves. **Coefficient alpha** is a type of internal consistency reliability that avoids the problem of having to decide how to split a scale into two halves. Done with computers, coefficient alpha is the same as an average of all the correlations of every possible division of the scale into two parts.

Which type of reliability a test requires depends on the nature of the characteristic being measured. Test-retest reliability is appropriate when the characteristic is stable over time. Alternate form reliability requires that an equivalent scale is developed, and internal consistency requires that the scale is measuring a single concept.

Test-Retest Reliability

An obvious type of reliability deals with the stability of test scores over time and is found by administering the same test to the same people on two different occasions. This is called **test-retest reliability** or temporal stability. This method of reliability determination is appropriate if one can assume that what is being measured remains fairly stable over time. If we had a test that could measure the anxiety a person experiences at a specific moment, we would not expect much test-retest reliability because of the many ups and downs people experience in their level of anxiety. We would need to use a different method of reliability for describing an anxiety test. However, many characteristics such as intelligence and academic ability, personality scales, work values, and sensory acuity variables are relatively stable over time, so test-retest reliability is a reasonable consideration for scales measuring such characteristics.

No test, even of a very stable variable, should be expected to demonstrate perfect test-retest reliability, because there are many factors that influence scores besides whatever it is we are trying to measure. Among these are

- differences in the state of the person when tested on the two occasions, like fatigue, concentration or mood;

- differences in the environmental conditions on the two occasions, such as noise and temperature;

74

- administration and scoring errors on the part of the examiner;

- changes in the people between administrations, such as new learning or development; and

- the fact that the first test may sensitize the subject to the second administration of the test, either increasing or decreasing the score. This sensitization includes both carryover effects—like the student taking a math test looking up answers he was unsure of after the first testing, so that his knowledge is in fact greater at the time of the second administration—as well as the subtle effects caused by people's reactions to having to take the same test over again.

Generally, the shorter the interval between the test and retest, the higher the reliability is, because true scores are less likely to change due to changes in the person within a shorter time span. However, carryover effects are more likely when the interval is very short, so intervals of at least two weeks between administrations are common. In evaluating reports of test-retest reliability in a test manual or article, pay close attention to the interval between administrations. Is the interval reasonable considering the test? What is being measured and what are the circumstances you can anticipate in your use of the instrument?

The number of scales included in the test may also affect test-retest reliability. With the MBTI instrument, the report of a personality type is the result of measurements on four independent scales. To have perfect test-retest reliability, we need to repeat the results on each of the four dichotomous scales.

To illustrate this complication, consider a young couple who decide they would like to have four children, and they would like all four to be boys. An adventurous couple, to say the least! What is the probability of their four children all being boys? The probability that the first child will be a boy is .50; the probability of the second child being a boy is also .50, and the same applies to child three and child four. What is the probability of all four of these events coming true? To find the joint probability of independent events like this, we must multiply each of the separate events, so

$$p = .50 \times .50 \times .50 \times .50 = .0625$$

Now, let's suppose we have a test with four scales, all of which must yield the same prediction for us to have the same results on retest. Further, let's suppose our test is so good that its test-retest reliability coefficient is an incredible .95. Because .95 is a correlation coefficient, we must square it for variance accounted for, to put it in percentage terms. When we square .95, we get .90. Thus, the probability of getting the same results on four highly reliable but independent scales is

$$p = .90 \times .90 \times .90 \times .90 = .66$$

The reliabilities of the MBTI assessment scales are not quite that high, but are between .90 and .95. The fact that experience shows about 75% of respondents taking the MBTI assessment come out the same type on retest is quite good considering the obstacle of having to make four separate predictions.

Alternate Form Reliability

Alternate form reliability, sometimes called *parallel form* or *equivalent form reliability*, is similar to test-retest reliability except that another form of the test, with all or nearly all different items, is administered in the second session. The main advantage of this type of reliability is that sensitization effects from having to take the items a second time are avoided, and there is no carryover effect from remembering things from the first testing session. Another advantage is that the two administrations can occur close to each other in time, so that new learning and other changes within the test taker are minimized. However, all the other sources of error that we had in test-retest reliability estimates are still present, such as differences in the state of the person or environmental conditions between the two test administrations, new learning or other changes in the people, scoring errors, and so forth. In addition, we have a new problem. Can we be certain the items in the two forms are really equivalent?

Because many instruments have a variety of forms, based on numerous revisions over time, one might think alternate form reliability could be quite easily accomplished. The problem is that alternate form reliability requires that the two forms have essentially no item overlap, while the reality is that most revisions of

---

Learning Key

Reliability: How consistently a test measures what it attempts to measure.

Test-retest reliability: Stability of test scores over time, measured by administering the same test to the same people on two different occasions and correlating the results.

Alternate form reliability: Stability over time, measured by administering different but equivalent forms of the same test to the same people on two different occasions and correlating the results.

Internal consistency reliability: Degree of consistency across items to see if a scale is measuring the same thing throughout. Determination requires only one administration of the test. There are two common kinds of internal consistency reliability:

    Split-half reliability: Dividing a scale into two halves and correlating them.

    Coefficient alpha: Computer provides the same thing as an average correlation of all possible splits of items into two halves.

common tests use many of the same items, or modify them only slightly. Because of the difficulty in developing two separate effective forms of a test, and then being sure they are really equivalent, alternate form reliability is rarely used except in situations where alternate forms are needed anyway. For example, certain achievement tests, such as the Woodcock-Johnson and the Wide Range Achievement Test, have alternate forms and some national testing programs for college or professional school entrance and licensing, such as the Scholastic Assessment Test (SAT) and Graduate Record Exam (GRE) need more than one form of the test, and are able to report alternate form reliability.

Internal Consistency Reliability

Alternate form reliability eliminates one of the problems of test-retest reliability—subjects having to respond to the same questions another time. **Internal consistency reliability** eliminates another problem: the need for the test developer to give the test a second time. Test takers in the standardization sample take the test once, and there is no need for concern about getting people to come back a second time or about what life experiences the people might have had that could affect their responses on the second occasion. (Please note that as a test user, you typically give a test to a person only once; this advantage of internal consistency reliability needing only one test administration applies to the test developer, who needs to give the test only once to standardization groups to establish reliability.) As the name implies, we are looking to see if each scale is internally consistent. Is each scale measuring the same thing throughout all the items? Internal consistency reliability does not measure stability over time, as test-retest reliability does, but estimates the degree of consistency across items. We will consider two forms of internal consistency reliability: split-half reliability and coefficient alpha.

Split-half Reliability

Split-half reliability is like alternate form reliability because it is produced by dividing a scale into two halves so that the items in one half are different from the items in the other half but are presumed to be equivalent. After the test is administered, we correlate the scores from items in one half of the scale with scores from the other half of the scale.

One problem with this method is deciding how best to split the items into two halves. Several different approaches have been used. A frequently used method is to correlate odd-numbered items with even-numbered items. Another approach is to use consecutive split halves in which the first half of the items is correlated with the items in the second half of the scale. This can be used only if a test is not a speed test and if the items are not in order of difficulty. Sometimes test developers logically split each scale of their test into two halves by pairing items that resemble each other and are highly correlated, placing one item of each pair in the first half and the other item in the second half. Yet another approach is to randomly assign items to the two halves. Perhaps the best approach to splitting the items is a combination of these last two approaches. In matched random subsets, two statistics are calculated for each item. The first statistic is the proportion of people who get the correct answer and the second statistic is the correlation of the item with the score on the total scale. Items that are similar to each other on those two statistics are placed in pairs, and one of each pair is chosen randomly to be in each half.

In a test with good internal consistency, the actual method of splitting the items may not be that crucial. In the 1998 MBTI revision, split-half studies were done using consecutive split-halves, logical split-halves, and comparing phrase questions and word pairs, and interestingly the results were good with each method, with very similar values above .90.

Split-half reliability studies often use the *Spearman-Brown prophecy* formula to correct for the fact that a half-size scale cannot achieve as high a reliability coefficient as a full-size scale. If we start with a 100-item test and split it into two halves, we are correlating two 50-item tests, rather than correlating a 100-item test with another 100-item test, as we would in test-retest reliability. Because reliability coefficients tend to be smaller for shorter tests, split-half reliabilities may be lower than other reliability estimates. The Spearman-Brown prophecy formula correction estimates what the correlation would be if the number of items had not been reduced. The estimated correlation is equal to $2r \div (1+r)$, where r represents the correlation of the two halves. Tables in test manuals will indicate when the Spearman-Brown correction has been used.

Another use of the Spearman-Brown formula is to see how adding items to a scale could increase its reliability. As we noted earlier, longer scales are usually more reliable. Suppose a scale has a reliability of .70; doubling the number of items of similar quality to the original items would likely increase the reliability to .82. Applying the Spearman-Brown formula above, we find $r = 2(.7) \div (1 + .7) = 1.4/1.7 = .82$.

Coefficient Alpha

Coefficient alpha, or Cronbach's alpha, is a frequently used type of internal consistency reliability that avoids the problem of having to decide how to split a scale into two halves. While the formula is based on item variances, coefficient alpha is essentially the same as if we had divided the scale into every possible division of two parts, found the correlation each time between the two halves, and then took an average of all these correlations. Because it is done with computers, it is easily accomplished and relieves the test creator of having to devise a scheme for dividing the items. The coefficient alpha formula automatically includes the Spearman-

Brown correction. Experience has shown little or no difference between coefficients using the split-half method from those using coefficient alpha when applied to good tests, so the ease of using coefficient alpha makes it widely used as a measure of internal consistency. *The Kuder-Richardson Formula 20* is similar to coefficient alpha, used when test items have only dichotomous answers, such as yes–no, true–false.

Evaluating Reliability

As you evaluate tests and procedures, you will want to note which kind of reliability is reported. You will want to know which kind of reliability is best for the test you are evaluating, test-retest or internal consistency reliability. The key is whether the characteristic being measured has stability over time. If the characteristic can be expected to be stable over time—like intelligence, ability, or personality—then test-retest (or alternate form) is appropriate. Internal consistency is the kind of reliability we expect to be reported when temporal stability is not expected in characteristics we are measuring—like anxiety or depression. Many test publishers will try to establish both kinds of reliability when possible.

You may wonder what constitutes "good" reliability. This will vary with the situation in which the instrument will be used. Remember that reliability is reported with correlation coefficients. As a general rule, reliabilities of about .70 to .80 are considered satisfactory for instruments being used in research, where the investigator is looking for general trends, not looking at the individuals themselves in the research. When our interest is in individual results, reliabilities of at least .80 tend to be considered satisfactory for screening purposes, but for diagnostic purposes a test's reliability should be at least .90. Obviously, what is being assessed will make a difference in what can be expected. Very high reliabilities are possible in highly focused areas, such as intelligence, while similar reliabilities are unlikely in less focused areas, such as creativity.

In interpreting test scores to individuals, a useful index of reliability is provided by the standard error of measurement and confidence intervals, which we consider next.

Standard Error of Measurement

Another way to look at the reliability of a test is through the standard error of measurement and confidence intervals. The **standard error of measurement** (SE_{meas}) yields information similar to the reliability coefficient but in terms that specifically apply to interpretation of an individual's score.

Overview

The **standard error of measurement** and **confidence intervals** are another way to look at the reliability of a test. The standard error of measurement estimates the standard deviation of the scores if a person were to take the same test over and over again. The percentages-of-cases information for the normal curve allows us to determine a confidence interval within which a person's true score is likely to fall at a given probability level.

The SE_{meas} estimates the standard deviation of the scores if a single person were to take the same test over and over again. We assume the person has no learning from the test or during the intervals between taking the test again and again.

If a person were to take a test a large number of times, the person would not get the same score each time but rather would get a distribution of scores. Measurement theory tells us that this distribution

- would be normal in shape,
- would have a mean equal to the person's true score, and
- would have a standard deviation that is estimated by the standard error of measurement.

Figure 4.1 presents a visual way to look at the SE_{meas}. The larger distribution in the figure represents the scores of all the people who take the test. In this example, the SD for all people taking the test is 8.5. The smaller shaded distribution is the distribution of scores of just one individual taking the test many times. While there is less variability for this one person than for all persons taking the test, there still is variability, and this SD of 3.0 is the standard error of measurement.

We don't actually need to have one person take the test over and over many times. We find the SE_{meas} by using the formula

$$SE_{meas} = SD_x \sqrt{1 - r_{xx}}$$

SD_x is the standard deviation of Test X, and r_{xx} is the reliability coefficient of Test X. There are two x's in the subscript because in a reliability coefficient we are correlating variable X with itself—with a retest, another form, or another half.

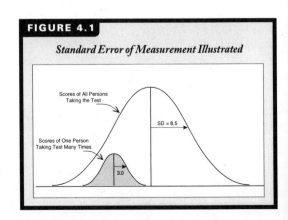

FIGURE 4.1

Standard Error of Measurement Illustrated

Scores of All Persons Taking the Test

SD = 8.5

Scores of One Person Taking Test Many Times

3.0

In an actual testing situation, we have only one obtained score for the person. That score is an estimate of the true score—and probably a fairly good estimate, even though we will never know what the true score for the person actually is. But we may wonder how much this person's obtained score is likely to differ from the true score.

When we focus on a range of scores within which we think the true score will be, we create a **confidence interval**, and the score values at the top and bottom of this range will be *confidence limits*. Because the distribution of scores we'd get if we gave the test over and over is a normal distribution, we can use the percentages-of-cases information shown in figure 2.7 on page 23. We know that 95% of cases will fall between 1.96 SD above and 1.96 SD below the mean. Thus the probability is .95 that the obtained score is no more than 1.96 SE_{meas} above or below the mean of the distribution of possible scores, which is our best guess for the true score. The score values at +1.96 times the SE_{meas} and -1.96 times the SE_{meas} are the 95% confidence limits.

For example, suppose we give a test and we know the SE_{meas} for the test is 3. The person receives a score of 100 on the test. We can find the 95% confidence limits by (a) multiplying the SE_{meas} by 1.96 and (b) adding and subtracting that amount from our obtained score of 100. Because our SE_{meas} is 3, and 3 times 1.96 is 5.88, we subtract 5.88 from 100 to get 94.12 as the lower limit of our confidence interval, and we add 5.88 to 100 to get 105.88 as the upper limit. We would be confident at the 95% level that the true score for our person would be between 94.12 and 105.88. Confidence limits can be set for any level of confidence we want, depending on how certain we want or need to be. A 90% confidence interval would be ±1.65 SE_{meas}, while a 99% confidence interval would be ±2.58 SE_{meas}.

You are already familiar with confidence intervals but may not have realized it. When you hear the results of a public opinion poll, for example, 52% approve of the president's performance, plus or minus 2.5%, the pollster is giving a confidence interval that the president's true public approval rating would fall between 49.5% and 54.5%; we just are not told what level of confidence is being used. The 2.5%

Learning Key

Standard error of measurement: Estimates the SD of a distribution of scores if a person were to take a test many, many times. Calculated using the SD and reliability coefficient of a test, it is an alternative way to look at a test's reliability.

Confidence interval: Range of scores within which the true score should fall, given a stated probability; based on the standard error of measurement.

margin of error could be 1 SE_{meas}, or it could be 1.65 times the SE_{meas}, or it could be 1.96 times the SE_{meas}, depending on whether the pollster was using a 68%, 90%, or 95% level of confidence. We are not given enough information to know how they arrived at the 2.5% margin of error.

Many tests, especially ability and aptitude tests, provide SE_{meas} or confidence interval information in their manuals so that a test administrator can provide this kind of reliability information to consumers. Suppose Johnny's parents ask the school counselor about the IQ of 105 Johnny received. Knowing that the SE_{meas} for the test Johnny took is 2.5 allows the counselor to tell the parents that we can be 95% certain his IQ falls between 100 and 110 (1.96 times 2.5 is 4.9). Confidence intervals are similar to significance levels we saw in chapter 3. When a result is significant at the .05 level, we can be 95% confident that the result did not happen by chance. If we have 95% confidence limits, we are 95% confident that the true score falls within the range. While professional decisions are often made based on an observed score, it is generally not appropriate to interpret a single observed score to a client. Rather, it is better to report a range of scores within which the true score is likely to lie. So, in our example above, it would be better to tell Johnny's parents that we can be 95% certain his IQ falls between 100 and 110 and never mention the 105. It might be even better to say Johnny falls in the upper half of the average range or to talk in terms of percentiles.

Reliability of Change Scores

Test users are sometimes interested in looking at change or difference scores, comparing a test result with another test or another administration of the same test. For example, one might want to compare the achievement score a person received at the beginning of a school year with that person's performance on the same test at the end of the year. Alternatively, on an instrument with multiple scales, one might be interested in comparing one scale with another scale. For example, we could see if a person's anxiety score were higher than his depression score, or see if a reading score were higher than a math score. Change or difference scores are typically calculated by subtracting the z-score of the one testing from the z-score of the other. For example, we could subtract the z-score of an individual on a reading test given at the beginning of the school year from the z-score of the person on the same test at the end of the year. We then would have a measure of the progress the person made during the year. Or we could subtract a math z-score from a reading z-score to have a measure of a possible discrepancy in achievement.

While each of the tests in these examples may have had good reliability, it is important to be aware that the reliability of change or difference scores is typically lower than the reliability of the original measures, often much lower.

This lower reliability of change scores compared to that of the tests on which they are based is the result of two factors: First, the *error* in each of the individual tests has an effect on the change score. Recall our discussion at the beginning of the chapter about an obtained score including both true score and error. When two tests are compared, the change score absorbs error from both tests. Second, the more the two tests are correlated with each other, the lower the reliability of the change score because whatever is common in the two tests tends to be canceled out when the change score is calculated.

The reliability of a change score can be estimated by subtracting the correlation between the tests from the average of the two individual test reliabilities, then dividing the result by 1 minus the correlation between the tests. This is represented in the formula:

$$r = \frac{\frac{1}{2}\,(r_{xx} + r_{yy}) - r_{xy}}{1 - r_{xy}}$$

where r_{xx} is the reliability of the first test, r_{yy} is the reliability of the second test, and r_{xy} is the correlation between the two tests.

As an example, suppose we have two tests with reliabilities of .90 and .70, and the correlation between the two tests is .60, the reliability of the change scores would be .50. Using the formula, .80 (the average of .90 and .70) minus .60 equals .20; we divide .20 by 1 minus .60 (which is .40) to get the .50 result. You really don't need to concern yourself with this formula. What is important to know is that anytime you are using change scores to compare performance on one testing with another testing, or between one subtest and another, you need to be cautious because the reliability of the change score may be much lower than you expect, even though the tests themselves are quite reliable.

Item Response Theory

Test-retest reliability and internal consistency reliability are traditional methods of looking at a test's measurement precision, or how free it is from error. **Item response theory (IRT)** is a newer approach to test precision that was used in the 1998 MBTI instrument revision.

Overview

A newer approach to test precision is called **item response theory (IRT)**. This approach looks at the relationship between a person's total score and the likelihood of making a particular response on an individual item. IRT shows the level of precision of a test in graph form instead of as a single reliability number. IRT looks at effectiveness of a given item by plotting an **item characteristic curve (ICC)** that shows precision across all points along a measurement scale. IRT can also be used to examine possible gender, age, or ethnic bias in an item or on a scale.

In traditional reliability approaches, we have a *single* estimate of the test's reliability for a given group. We may give the test to the group on one occasion and again on another occasion, and come up with one correlation coefficient for the two sets of scores. The correlation coefficient is an index of how reliable the test is over time. We could also split the items or use coefficient alpha to tell us how consistent the test is within itself.

These reliability coefficients based on correlations give us a single number, which represents the reliability across the entire scale, without expecting precision to be different at different points along the scale. However, studies have shown that coefficients based on correlations tend to over-estimate precision on extreme scores and under-estimate precision on scores near the midpoint.

IRT approaches, on the other hand, assume that a test probably will be more precise at some points along the scale than at other points. Instead of having a single reliability number, IRT shows the level of precision of a test in *graph* form.

IRT focuses on the relationship between a person's true score on the characteristic being measured and the likelihood of making a particular response to an individual test item. True score is suggested by the total score the person gets on the whole scale. To illustrate, let's consider a possible Extraversion–Introversion item, "talkative" versus "quiet." How likely is it that a person who really has an Introversion preference (based on the total E–I scale) will choose the "quiet" Introversion response on our item?

To look at the effectiveness of a given item, we plot an **item characteristic curve (ICC)**, illustrated in figure 4.2, which has ICCs for two imaginary items. An ICC is a graph that shows us how effective an item is, and in what way. Usually these curves are created by computer programs and are based on the test results from many people.

In IRT, an individual's score is called *theta* (θ), and different levels of θ are plotted along the baseline of the item characteristic curve. Don't let the Greek word theta throw you; think continuous score or just score. As in all graphs in statistics, low scores are at the left end of the baseline and high scores are to the right. For the MBTI instrument, scores to the left of the midpoint on the baseline are scores of the Extraversion, Sensing, Thinking, or Judging preference, and to the right are scores in the Introversion, Intuition (N), Feeling, or Perceiving direction. Scores at the far left of the scale would show a very clear preference of E, S, T, or J. Moving to the right; we would see decreasingly clear preferences until we get to the midpoint, when we see increasingly clear preferences for I, N, F, or P.

In IRT, the right side is called the *keyed direction*, so I, N, F or P are the keyed direction for each of their dichotomies. As θ (theta) increases from left to right on the baseline, we expect that there is a greater likelihood a person will respond in the keyed direction. In other words, we expect a person with a clear preference for Introversion to have a higher likelihood of choosing "quiet" in our item than would a person with a clear preference for Extraversion. The probability of a "quiet" response will get higher the farther the person's total E–I score goes toward the right.

The vertical axis on our ICC plot is called *probability of a keyed response (pkr)*. Note in figure 4.2 that the pkr goes from 0.0 at the bottom to 1.0 at the top. The probability of answering an item in the keyed direction (toward I, N, F, or P) can go from very unlikely to almost certain. The first item graphed in figure 4.2 shows that the probability of a keyed response gets gradually higher as we move from left to right on the scale. With the second item, there is an abrupt transition in the pkr as we get to the midpoint. There is a zero likelihood of a keyed response with low scores up to almost the midpoint and a perfect 1.0 pkr from just past the midpoint to the far right of the graph. The ICC in the second graph is an ideal curve, doing exactly what we would want an item to do in discriminating between two dichotomous preferences. In actual practice, of course, no item is ideal.

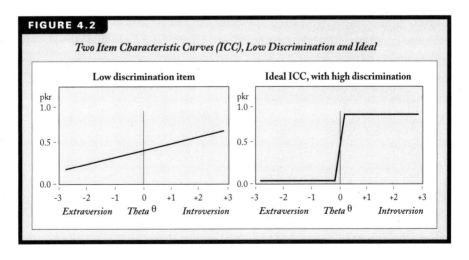

FIGURE 4.2

Two Item Characteristic Curves (ICC), Low Discrimination and Ideal

In an IRT of the type used with the MBTI instrument, there are three *parameters* describing an item characteristic curve for each item. The parameters define the way in which scores relate to the likelihood of answering the item in the keyed direction. These parameters are designated *a*, *b*, and *c*.

The *a parameter* describes the item's *discrimination*, the steepness in the slope of the curve. We look to see if there is a steep slope somewhere on the curve, a place where the curve suddenly rises sharply from the bottom base line to the top line. For example, is there a fairly clear point at which respondents choose the Introversion response rather than the Extraversion response? Comparing the two items in figure 4.2, it is obvious that the ideal item in the second graph has a greater *a parameter*, that is, its slope is steep rather than gradual. Generally, the steeper the curve, the more *information* or measurement precision is provided. If the curve is flat, there is no information and our item is not discriminating; the probability of the person responding in the keyed direction is the same or nearly the same at any point along the scale.

If our "talkative" versus "quiet" item is discriminating well, there will come a point on the scale as we move from left to right where there will be a fairly sudden shift from those who mark "talkative" to those who mark "quiet." We will have a steep slope that demonstrates discrimination is occurring on this item. However, if there is little relationship between total E–I scores and responses to this item, so that lots of Extraverts mark "quiet" or lots of Introverts mark ""talkative," our discrimination will be low, and our curve will be more flat. In figure 4.2, the first item does discriminate some, but not very effectively.

The second parameter in an ICC, called the *b parameter* or *difficulty* parameter, tells us how hard or easy it is to answer the item in the keyed direction. We look to see where on the scale, from left to right, the steep part of the slope is located. The hard and easy terms in relation to the *b parameter* may make more sense if we consider an item on a quiz. If a quiz item is hard, only the people who studied really well get the correct answer, and most people miss it. We will expect the greatest amount of slope not at the midpoint but nearer the right end of the baseline. Discrimination is between the few very best students and the larger remainder of

Learning Key

Item response theory (IRT): A method of developing and evaluating tests, showing measurement precision in graph form.

Item characteristic curve (ICC): Graph showing how effective a test item is across all points along a measurement scale.

the class. If an item is easy, only a few miss the item, and most get the item correct. The ICC's greatest slope is near the low end or the left side of the scale for an easy item.

Obviously, a personality instrument would not have a right or wrong answer. The difficulty parameter in this case represents the "difficulty" in responding with the answer that is designated as the keyed direction. With the MBTI instrument, we want the greatest slope to be close to the midpoint. If the steep part of the slope occurs near the midpoint, we assume the item is discriminating between even slight preferences for Extraversion and slight preferences for Introversion. In figure 4.3, the first ICC is for an item with good discrimination that occurs at the midpoint—even if it does not separate Extraverts and Introverts as cleanly as the ideal item in figure 4.2.

The second ICC in figure 4.3 has a slope similar to the first ICC in this figure, but the maximum discrimination of the item is shifted to the right of the midpoint. Because this is a shift to the right, this would be a hard or difficult item, as in the quiz example. This potential Extraversion–Introversion item displayed in the right graph of figure 4.3 has a high *b parameter*, which means its best separation would be between those who have a clear preference for Introversion and those with a not-so-clear Introversion preference (as well as all of those with an Extraversion preference). If the slope occurred much to the right of the midpoint, we would know that on that particular item, many respondents with an Introversion preference choose the response that indicates Extraversion. In a personality type instrument, we want the clear separation to be between Extraverts and Introverts, at the midpoint, as occurs in the first ICC in figure 4.3.

If our "talkative" versus "quiet" item discriminates well (a parameter) and does so near the midpoint (b parameter), we are on our way to an effective item.

FIGURE 4.3

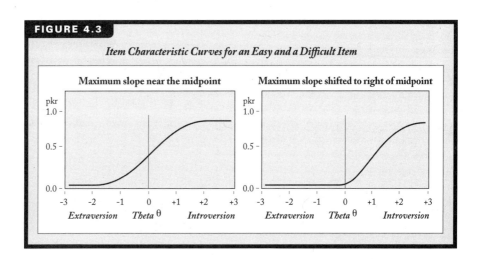

Item Characteristic Curves for an Easy and a Difficult Item

The third or *c parameter* is called the *lower asymptote* parameter and describes where the ICC curve flattens out for those who score at the left end of the scale. We look to see if the curve begins at the baseline. If the curve comes close to the baseline, we have a *zero lower asymptote*, but if the curve is somewhat above the baseline, we have a *nonzero asymptote*.

The importance of the c parameter may be easier to understand if we again consider a quiz. If our quiz is multiple choice, we would not expect anyone to get a score of zero, even if they hadn't studied or listened to the lectures, because they could guess and get some items right. Assuming each item has four choices, a particular item on this quiz might have a pkr close to .25 even for the poorest students, because by chance they could guess the right answer about 25% of the time. The ICC curve at the far left end of the graph could be above the .25 point above the baseline and we would not be concerned, because we know people can guess items correctly. However, if we are measuring preference for Extraversion or Introversion, we would not want 25% of people with a clear preference for Extraversion to be choosing the Introvert response. In an effective item the pkr for these people would be very close to 0.0. Expectations for what ICCs should look like vary with the kind of test that is being developed.

Turn back to figure 4.2. The first item in figure 4.2 has a lower asymptote problem. The ICC does not come down to the 0.0 point on the scale at the low end. This means that even people with a clear preference for Extraversion had a higher than 0 chance of answering this item in the Introverted direction.

With the MBTI instrument, we usually don't have people guessing, but we *do* have to be concerned with social desirability—or social *un*desirability—and other factors that might cause people to respond a particular way, even if that is not their true preference. Presence of a nonzero lower asymptote alerts a test developer to the possibility that something is present in the item that leads people to respond in the opposite direction from what is correct for them, for example that even clear Extraverts would respond in the Introverted direction. The *c parameter* helps identify what have been termed overpopular or socially desirable answers.

In constructing Form M of the MBTI instrument, IRT was used to assist in the selection of items for the instrument. The test developers selected items that have clear levels of slope on the a parameter, have their maximum discrimination near the midpoint (*b parameter*), and have curves that begin near the baseline (no *c parameter* problem).

It is also possible to determine if there are gender or age biases in an item by using *differential item functioning* (DIF). A standardization sample can be divided by gender, by age, by ethnicity, or by any other variable of concern. Then an ICC can be drawn to show characteristics of responses for each subgroup in the sample.

Figure 4.4 compares responses of males and females to an item being considered for inclusion in a test. The first graph has curves for males and females that are quite different. The item seems to work quite well for males, but there is little discrimination and a nonzero lower asymptote for females. We would have to conclude there is some kind of gender bias at work. In the second graph, males and females respond in very much the same manner, so there seems to be no gender bias in that item. DIF can be used to look at possible bias for a total scale as well as for individual items. In fact, slight variation between groups on individual items is not uncommon, but at the scale level we will hope these slight variations cancel each other out. While the ICC graph usually shows how an *individual item* functions, the *test information function* (TIF) shows how a *scale* functions. In simple terms, TIF can be thought of as the IRT equivalent of a reliability coefficient, though a reliability coefficient is a single number, and TIF is depicted in a graph that shows how much information is provided at each possible value of theta. In figure 4.5, the first graph illustrates a TIF for an instrument such as the MBTI personality tool where it is important that the most information (discrimination) occurs at the midpoint of the scale. Just as we saw that the ideal ICC has its greatest discrimination at the midpoint, we want the same for the total scale as plotted in the TIF. We are not interested in sorting sharply between Extraverts with a very clear preference clarity from those whose preference clarity is moderate. We do not need much information at the two ends of the baseline. What we *are* concerned with is separating Introverts from Extraverts, even when the preference clarity is slight. The TIF in figure 4.5 shows that the discriminative power of this instrument is primarily near the middle of the scale rather than the extremes, as is appropriate for the MBTI instrument.

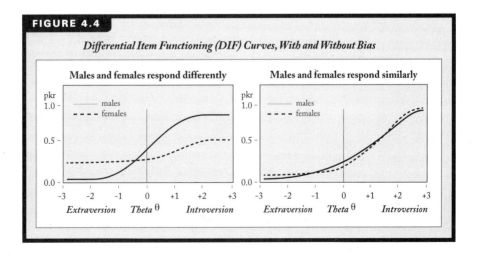

FIGURE 4.4

Differential Item Functioning (DIF) Curves, With and Without Bias

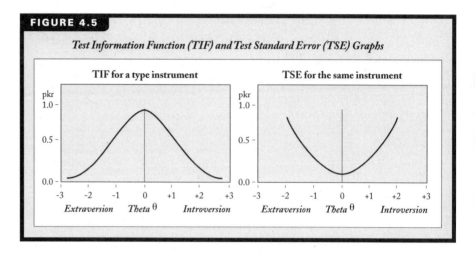

FIGURE 4.5

Test Information Function (TIF) and Test Standard Error (TSE) Graphs

The *test standard error* (TSE) is the IRT equivalent of the standard error of measurement. The TSE is presented in graph form and is, essentially, the mirror image of the TIF graph. For purposes of a test such as the MBTI instrument, we want the TSE graph to show the least amount of error at the midpoint. The second graph in figure 4.5 shows the TSE of the same test as displayed in the TIF graph. What we see is that there is the least amount of error near the midpoint, where we need precision, and more error as we move away from the midpoint.

With IRT a test developer can determine where it is most important to have the greatest information and select items that give good information at that point. Precision at the midpoint is essential for a type-sorting instrument, but suppose we have a test for the trait of anxiety. For anxiety, precision would be important not at the midpoint but somewhere higher on the scale, to help us differentiate people who might need mental health intervention from the majority of people who can get along without it.

IRT can also be used as the basis for computer scoring a test, as is done with Form M of the MBTI instrument. IRT allows for effective weighting of items, so the best items receive more weight in the scoring than so-so items do, using the three parameters *a, b,* and *c* for each item. For example, an item with an ICC close to ideal might be expected to have a higher weight or predictive value than an item with a less ideal curve.

IRT is not as widely known in the world of test development and evaluation, but there is great potential for broader use of this method in the years to come.

Exercises and Questions to Check Your Understanding

1. Reliability of test results may be affected by

    A. Fatigue and changes in mood

    B. New learning between administrations

    C. Differences in the testing environment

    D. All of the above.

2. The goal of test-retest reliability is to

    A. Get 100% reliability

    B. Get a normal distribution

    C. Get consistent results in repeated administrations

    D. Get confirmation that we are measuring what we intend to measure

3. Place in the blank the letter(s) that identify the type(s) of reliability you would look for if you were selecting an instrument for each of these situations.

    a. test-retest

    b. alternate form

    c. internal consistency (split half, coefficient alpha)

    _____ A.   An intelligence test

    _____ B.   A test of stress levels–the kind that are highly changeable from time to time

    _____ C.   A test of anxiety–the kind that is pretty stable over time, such as chronic worry

    _____ D.   A test measuring core characteristics of personality

    _____ E.   A college entrance test used nation-wide, such as the SAT or ACT

    _____ F.   A test measuring response to change, such as in a business merger or organizational restructuring

4. Suppose we want to study the reliability of the XYZ Inventory. We give the XYZ Inventory to several groups and find the following data:

Test-Retest Correlations of XYZ Inventory Continuous Scores

Sample	Interval	N	r
High school Seniors	2 weeks	85	.65
University sophomores	2 weeks	94	.75
University sophomores	2 months	78	.69
University sophomores	6 months	65	.60
Middle-aged high school graduates	2 weeks	79	.79
Middle-aged university graduates	3 weeks	80	.86

A. What kind of reliability does this data represent? _____

_____

B. What effect does age have on reliability of XYZ scores? _____

_____

C. What impact does amount of education seem to have on the reliability of

the XYZ? _____

_____

D. How does the interval between test and retest effect reliability of the

XYZ? _____

_____

E. How much variance is accounted for by the weakest correlation in this

data? _____

5. **Three of the following are true about the standard error of measurement. Which one is not?**

_____ A.   The standard error of measurement is related to the reliability of the test.

_____ B.   The standard error of measurement estimates the standard deviation of the scores of a person taking the same test over and over again.

_____ C.   The standard error of measurement identifies the sources of error in our measurement.

_____ D.   The standard error of measurement helps us create confidence levels within which a person's true score should fall.

6. Johnny took a mechanical aptitude test and received a score of 103. The SE_{meas} for this test is 2.10. Between what two values can we be 95% certain that Johnny's true score on mechanical aptitude would be? Approximation is fine.

between _____ and _____

7. Item characteristic curves in IRT provide a way to evaluate effectiveness of an item at various points along the scale. For each of the four ICCs, choose the description that best fits what the graph is showing.

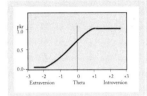 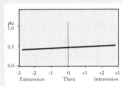 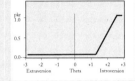 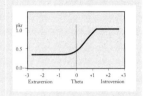

_____ _____ _____ _____

A. No discrimination (no information); item does not separate groups

B. Good discrimination, but item is "difficult"; separation is between people with very high scores and all the others (between moderate and clear Is, not between Es and Is)

C. Good discrimination, but item is "easy"; separation is between people with very low scores and all the others (between clear and moderate Es, not between Es and Is)

D. Fair discrimination, but a large nonzero lower asymptote suggests the item may have a social desirability problem

5
Validity

In addition to being reliable, a good test must also be valid. Validity refers to how well a test measures what it is intended to measure. Unlike establishing reliability, which is a fairly straightforward process, seeking validity is a complex process. Establishing validity involves both

- the convergence of many studies, and
- examination of the test from several different perspectives.

In this chapter we will focus on three aspects of evidence for validity. Then we will discuss validity coefficients, and we will look at the statistical techniques of factor analysis and latent class analysis. Finally, we will discuss the relationship between reliability and validity, and between validity and professional use of a test.

Evidence for Validity

Validity refers to how well a test measures what it is intended to measure. The complex process of establishing a test's validity utilizes three types of information: content-related, criterion-related, and construct-related evidence for validity.

Overview

Content-related evidence for validity is provided by expert judges who evaluate the test content to determine if the items really measure only the content the test is supposed to measure, if they cover all of the content domain, and if they are at an appropriate difficulty level. **Face validity**, what a test superficially appears to measure, is sometimes confused with content validity. Having a test appear reasonable and appropriate to potential test-takers may be desirable, but for many tests face validity is not critical.

In **criterion-related evidence for validity**, a test is compared with an established benchmark or criterion. The criterion is an independent measure of the characteristic the test is designed to measure. The criterion may be scores from another test, or it may be an observable behavior that is recognized as measuring the characteristic. There are two types of criterion-related validity, which differ primarily in when the criterion is measured. In **concurrent validity**, test scores are compared with the person's current performance on the criterion. For **predictive validity**, test scores are compared with behavior or scores on a criterion that need, by their nature, to be measured some time in the future.

Construct-related evidence for validity relates to the psychological meaningfulness of a test. Construct-related validity is determined by defining the **construct**—the theoretical idea or concept—being measured, and by examining how the test relates to the construct and to other measures theoretically related to the construct. This kind of validity is established by a gradual process of accumulating evidence from many sources to determine the nature of the characteristic and whether that is what the test is measuring. A test that has construct validity should correlate highly with other tests or measures of the same characteristic or other theoretically related characteristics. This is called **convergent validity**. A test should also have low correlations with measures of characteristics we would theoretically expect to be different. This is called **discriminant validity**. *Both* convergent and discriminant evidence are necessary for a test to have good construct-related validity.

In real-world test validation, content-, criterion- and construct-related validity are not treated separately, though each may be important to establishing the validity of a test.

The complex process of establishing the **validity** of a test involves examination of three types of information: content-related validity, criterion-related validity, and construct-related validity. All of these are aspects of a test's effectiveness in measuring what it is intended to measure. They are not compartmentalized components, but instead are aspects of a unitary concept representing all of the evidence supporting the intended use of the test. Both the test developer and the test user need to look at validity holistically. However, for our purposes, we will look at the three approaches separately so we understand what validity involves.

Content-Related Evidence for Validity

Content-related validity, sometimes referred to as content relevance or content coverage, is evaluated through careful examination by judges of the content of a test. It is established by

- examining the appropriateness of the items included and asking whether each item really measures the content the test is supposed to measure,

- judging the completeness of the item sample to see how well the test covers the domain or topic it is supposed to cover, and

- determining whether the level of mastery at which the content is assessed is appropriate.

The process of determining the content aspect of validity relies heavily on expert evaluation. This kind of evidence is particularly important for tests of achievement or ability. A person taking a college entrance exam, such as the SAT, will want the content to cover appropriately the content that is typical for high school students. If you are taking a course, we will hope the exam you take at the end of the class will have good content validity. We hope such an exam will do the following:

- Sample the content covered in the course and not ask questions about another subject.

- Representatively sample all the material covered, so all the questions are not about just one topic from the course.

- Be at an appropriate level of difficulty, not asking questions even the experts would have trouble answering, or not being so easy that you feel you wasted your time studying for the exam.

Content-related aspects of validity are important for tests of achievement or ability. They are less a concern for tests of personality and mental health, where high content validity could limit the overall usefulness of the test. The purpose of a personality test is to identify characteristics in people's personalities. Whether the items cover a content domain related to that characteristic is not important. We are more interested in whether the items effectively identify *if* the characteristic is present or *to what degree* it is present in the person. In fact, in some cases we may not want the person to know what it is we are looking for, such as when we are looking for signs of depression or another mental disorder in a mental health test.

Content-related validity sometimes has been confused with **face validity**, which deals not with what a test measures but with what it superficially *appears* to measure. Technically face validity really is not validity at all. It is more a matter of rapport and public relations. All other things being equal, it is good for a test to *look* valid, to appear reasonable and appropriate to potential test-takers and other observers. Face validity may affect the test-taker's attitude, level of cooperation, honesty, and so forth, but in the long run, technical validity is far more important. Some instruments, because of their purpose, avoid having face validity.

Criterion-Related Evidence for Validity

Criterion-related validity deals with comparing a test with an *established* benchmark or criterion. If we were in the yardstick manufacturing business and we wanted to assure that our yardsticks were valid measures of length, our criterion would be the standard foot at the National Bureau of Standards. If a set of measurements with a sample of our yardsticks corresponded closely—that is, were highly correlated and had similar means and standard deviations—with a set of measurements using the standard foot, we would conclude our yardsticks were a valid measure of length.

For a psychological instrument, the criterion is an independent measure of the characteristic the test is designed to measure. It may be scores from another, already established test or it may be data from an observable behavior that is recognized as measuring the characteristic. Depending on the purpose of the test, an appropriate criterion might be, for example, school grades, supervisors' ratings,

---

Learning Key

Validity: How well a test measures what it is intended to measure.

Content-related evidence for validity: Items on a test measure only relevant content, at an appropriate difficulty level, and adequately sample the content area to be measured.

Face validity: Test measures what it *appears* to measure.

Criterion-related evidence for validity: Test correlates with an established benchmark or criterion, such as an observable behavior or another established test measuring the same characteristic. If the criterion is measured at the same time as the new test, it is called **concurrent validity**; if the criterion will be measured in the future, it is called **predictive validity**.

Construct-related evidence for validity: A test is psychologically meaningful; it relates to the theoretical concept or idea the test intends to measure. Includes two sub-types, both of which are essential:

> **Convergent** validity: Test correlates with other measures of the same or related theoretical concepts or constructs.

> **Discriminant** validity: Test does not correlate with measures of different constructs.

Construct: A theoretical idea constructed from a variety of observable indicators into a unified concept.

number or dollar amount of sales, diagnostic classification, or performance on another test.

The choice of a criterion is very important. If we had a new intelligence test, we would compare the results with an established intelligence measure like the Stanford-Binet Intelligence Scale or the Wechsler Adult Intelligence Scale. If we had a new test for depression, we would compare the results with the established Beck Depression Inventory. If we had a new test of Jungian personality types, we'd compare the results with an established test for determining such types, such as the MBTI instrument. The key is having a criterion that is *established*—that is well researched and generally accepted—against which to compare the scale we want to validate. If a criterion is not well-known, a test publisher will need to provide independent evidence for the validity of the criterion as well as correlations to the test that is being validated.

There are two types of criterion-related validity evidence—concurrent and predictive—which differ primarily in when the criterion is measured. In **concurrent validity**, test scores are compared with the person's current performance on the criterion test or behavior. The test we are validating and the criterion would be measured in the same time period, perhaps at the very same testing session. For example, we could take physiological measures of anxiety while people are filling out our new anxiety scale, or we could give people an established anxiety inventory during the same session as they complete our new test.

For **predictive validity**, sometimes referred to as predictive utility, test scores are compared with behavior or scores on a criterion to be administered some time in the future to see how effective the test is in forecasting the future outcome. We could validate a test of reading readiness, for example, by giving it to a group of preschool children and correlating their scores with a valid reading achievement test given after they complete first grade, or we could compare SAT scores of high-school seniors with their grade-point-averages (GPAs) at the end of the freshman year of college. The criterion is administered later because time for development must occur before we can see if the test we are validating is able to predict how that future behavior will turn out.

It is important that the test publisher provide accurate and complete descriptions in the test manual of the measures or criteria used in validity studies so that test users can draw their own conclusions about the validity evidence and determine the relevance of the test for their applications.

Construct-Related Evidence for Validity

Construct-related validity is concerned with the psychological meaningfulness of a test. It is determined by

99

- defining as clearly as possible the construct to be measured, that is, the theoretical idea, the concept or the framework, and

- considering how the test relates to the construct and to other measures theoretically related to the construct.

You may wonder what this term **construct** is all about. The term *construct* relates to the fact that the concept we are attempting to measure is *constructed* by mental synthesis. We've never seen or touched a concept like anxiety, for example. The concept of anxiety has been constructed based on things we *can* observe, like nervous trembling, stammering, insomnia, and reported apprehension and discomfort. The construct brings together a variety of indicators into a unified concept. Other constructs, such as Extraversion, depression, or intelligence are concepts that have similarly been constructed from a variety of observable components into a single concept.

The construct-related validity of a test is not established by one successful prediction, but is a gradual process of accumulating evidence from many experiments and observations to determine the nature of the characteristic and whether that is what our test is really measuring.

A test that has construct-related validity should correlate highly with other tests or measures of the same characteristic or other theoretically related characteristics. This is called **convergent validity**. The correlations between these measures of the same construct show they *converge*, or narrow in, on the same thing. In a way, convergent validity is like criterion validity, in that scores on the test being validated are related to scores on some other measure. In convergent validity, however, there is no criterion for what it is we are attempting to measure, such as college grades that serve as the criterion for the predictive value of SAT scores. In convergent validity, the meaning of the test comes to be defined by the measures it is associated with. For example, there is no single criterion for Extraversion–Introversion, but correlations with measures of sociability, dominance, social presence, self-confidence, and internality help define the meaning of the dichotomy. Evidence that is provided for convergent validity helps us understand the construct that is measured by the test.

In addition to high correlations with other measures of the same construct, a test should also have *low correlations* with measures of characteristics that we would theoretically expect to be different. This is called **discriminant validity** or divergent validity. Very low correlations with measures of different or unrelated constructs demonstrate that the test is measuring only the construct that was intended. It is fine to have fairly strong correlations between Extraversion–Introversion and measures of sociability and dominance, but we also need low correlations between E–I and intelligence. Because Extraversion–Introversion is not supposed to be related to intelligence, if we find a moderate or high correlation between our E–I scale and an intelligence scale, then we know something is not as it should be.

While many test manuals focus primarily on demonstrating convergent validity, *both* convergent and discriminant validity evidence are necessary for a test to have good construct validity. If a hair care product says it is an anti-frizz gel, then we expect the product to work like other similar products that relax the frizziness of hair. At the same time, we want assurance that this anti-frizz product does *not* work like products that color the hair. We want convergent validity with hair care products that have the same or a similar purpose. We want discriminant validity with products that have a different purpose.

Accumulating convergent and discriminant validity evidence—correlating test scores with other variables we expect them to relate to, and making sure our test does not correlate with constructs it should not correlate with—is what most people think of as construct validity. That kind of evidence is important, but establishing the construct aspect of validity includes a variety of other processes as well, including:

- gathering experts' judgments that the content of the test relates to the construct we are trying to measure,

- analyzing the internal consistency of the test, and

- questioning test takers in detail about their responses to try to determine the specific processes they went through in arriving at those responses.

The first two points are similar to things we have looked at already. Gathering experts' judgments about the content of the test looks like content-related validity. It is similar, but here expert judgments about content are made to be sure the construct being measured is appropriately covered. This includes what are known as *construct under-representation* and *construct-irrelevant variance*. As the construct is fully explored, there may be aspects of the construct that are not adequately tapped by the test, which would be construct under-representation. For example, if an anxiety test does not cover adequately all aspects of the anxiety construct, including reported discomfort and apprehension but not the physiological aspects, its usefulness could be limited because all important components of the construct are not represented. Construct-irrelevant variance would include factors unrelated to the construct that influence scores, such as vocabulary that is not understandable to people taking the test. The focus of this content analysis is different from the usual content validity examination of an achievement or ability test, where the concern is adequate coverage of what the test taker needs to know. Here the concern of the content analysis is whether the test developer has an adequate definition of the construct.

In the process of developing the MBTI instrument, Myers studied the constructs of Extraversion and Introversion and identified several aspects that were part of the construct of each. As she developed test items, she made sure that she included several items related to each aspect. Her attention to the aspects of each construct not only assured coverage of the whole construct but also formed the basis of the facets in Step II of the instrument, in which there are five subscales for each of the personality dichotomies.

In the previous chapter we saw internal consistency as a reliability measure, but internal consistency also relates to construct validity. If our test is measuring a construct, and only that construct, it should have good internal consistency, that is, its items should be measuring one concept and should correlate well with each other.

Interviewing people who have taken the test to inquire why they responded as they did on each of the items can be helpful in understanding whether the items are measuring what the test developer intended, and what might make the items more effective in targeting the construct. This is one of the approaches Myers used in finding the most effective MBTI items. She interviewed a group of about 20 family and friends whose type she knew, asking about the responses they gave on new items she was trying out. In the process of developing the Indicator, she tried out more than 20,000 items to obtain the 93 items that are scored for the basic scales.

While we have looked at content-, criterion-, and construct-related validity evidence separately to help understand the components of the validation process, we need to remember the point made at the beginning of the chapter that types of validity are not separable in the real world. When we consider the evidence for the validity of a test, we are not interested in one type of validity but a combination of all three kinds of evidence. Because it is the most inclusive of the forms of validity, the term *construct validity* in some manuals and texts refers to the combination of content-, criterion-, and construct-related validity as we have considered them here.

Validity Coefficients

Just as we report reliability as a correlation coefficient, we also use the correlation coefficient to report most validity evidence. When we are looking at the reliability of a test, we are generally going to want tests to have reliabilities of at least .70, and preferably .80 and above. We remember that correlations must be squared to see what percentage of the variance they account for. A test with a test-retest or internal consistency reliability of .70 accounts for only 49% of the variance. Half of what the scores tell us is noise, relating to error. A reliability of .80 tells us that 64% of the scores relate to what we are measuring, and 36% is noise. Intelligence and achievement tests tend to have higher reliabilities, typically exceeding .90 and thus having less than 20% error. Obviously, the higher the reliability the better.

When it comes to validity, we will find much lower correlation coefficients. In reliability, we are seeing if our test is measuring a characteristic consistently, but in validity we are looking at relationships between the characteristic the test is measuring and other characteristics and behaviors. Both our test's unreliability, and the unreliability of the measures of other characteristics we are considering, compound to reduce our validity coefficients.

That is not all that keeps validity coefficients lower. We also need to remember that human behavior is very complex. No single characteristic accounts for more than a small part of the variability in what people do. One rarely sees validity coefficients above .60, and coefficients in the .30 and .40 range are often seen as quite good. Depending on the circumstances, a test that improves our understanding of, or ability to predict, a person's behavior by a small percentage, maybe 5 to 10%, may be quite worthwhile.

We should note that the problem of low validity coefficients is not unique to psychological and social measures. Many commonly used medical diagnostic tests have validity coefficients similar to those we find with behavioral measures, but when these medical tests are combined with other sources of data, they are able to aid in providing diagnostic clues. As in medicine, behavioral tests are seldom used alone, but are used by professionals in combination with other sources of information, such as interviews, histories, and outside reports.

Factor Analysis

As you review validity evidence in test manuals, you will frequently find reference to factor analysis. Factor analysis is a statistical technique that simplifies complex sets of data. It is often used in test development and in studies to establish the construct validity of a test.

Overview

Factor analysis is a statistical technique, often used in validity studies, that simplifies complex sets of data. All items in a test are correlated with each other, and from those correlations the factor analysis computer program pulls common elements, or **factors**, and provides factor loadings, a kind of correlation of each item with each factor. Alternatively, a factor analysis may take correlations between a group of different tests to see how they relate to each other.

To understand what factor analysis is all about, let's consider a simple example. Suppose we open a small diner. We have limited funds and experience, so our menu has only these nine items:

Bratwurst	Sauerkraut
Chow mein	Sopaipillas
Egg foo yung	Strudel
Enchiladas	Wonton soup
Frijoles	

As people place their orders, we observe that the menu items tend to fall into three groups. Most people who order bratwurst also order sauerkraut and strudel. They don't tend to order chow mein or enchiladas with bratwurst. When someone orders chow mein, they are likely also to order egg foo yung and wonton soup. Enchiladas, frijoles, and sopaipillas tend to go together. Observing these patterns, we look for what these groupings of menu items have in common. We may observe that the common element among the items in the first group is that they are all German foods, while the common element among items in the second group is that they are Chinese foods, and the third are Mexican foods.

In statistics the term we use for the common element is **factor**. If we did a factor analysis on the menu choices in our diner, we would probably get three factors, each one related to one of the three cuisines, confirming what we discovered in just looking at our data.

Suppose we have a 100-item personality test and want to know what personality variables the test really measures, not just what the authors say it measures. Because there are too many items for us to just look over and see the relationships as we did with our menu items, factor analysis helps us find common factors among the items. First, we would give the test to a large number of people and have the answer sheets computer scored. Next, we would correlate each item with every other item in the test. We would have the correlation of Item 1 with Item 2, Item 2 with Item 3, Item 1 with Item 3, etc., across *all* items in the test. The factor analysis starts with these correlations and determines which correlations go together across all the people who took the test. The computer programs that do the factor analysis try to find the smallest number of factors needed to account for the most differences among these items.

Factor analysis computes factor loadings, a kind of correlation of each item with each factor. We look at the factor loadings and label the factors based on the nature of the items that have the highest loadings (correlations) on that factor. For example, one group of items that go together may be labeled Extraversion–Introversion because that is what the items loading on the factor seem to be measuring, and another group of items may be labeled Sensing–Intuition. In this example we correlated individual test items, but factor analysis can also be used to correlate whole tests or scales to see how the different measures relate to each other.

There are two broad types of factor analysis: exploratory and confirmatory. *Exploratory factor analysis* tries to explore a field, discovering the main constructs or dimensions out of a complex set of data. That was the purpose of the very first factor analysis in 1904, when Spearman tried to investigate what constructs (theoretical concepts) could account for the correlations between human abilities. The concept of general intelligence developed from this work.

Another kind of factor analysis is called *confirmatory analysis*. We use this when we are able to hypothesize what we think factor loadings should be, based on previous research and on theory. Confirmatory factor analysis determines how good the fit is between some data and a theory about what that data should look like. Studies reported in the MBTI manual that test whether the data support Jung's and Myers' theory of personality types are examples of this kind of factor analysis.

Many personality instruments have been developed by using exploratory factor analysis. A diverse group of personality test items are assembled, given to a large group, and then processed using the factor analysis method. Scales are then created from items that go together. The approach of beginning with a theory, then using confirmatory factor analysis to confirm that items and scales that are developed do in fact fit the theory is generally seen as superior to exploratory factor analysis when it comes to the development of personality measures. The resulting scales are more likely to have a meaningful relationship to each other.

Latent Class Analysis

Another statistical technique sometimes used in the development and validation of psychological tests is **latent class analysis (LCA),** which has some similarities to factor analysis. A latent class or latent variable is like a construct or a factor in that it cannot be directly observed itself, but rather it is inferred from other variables that are observed and directly measured. Latent classes allow the grouping of a number of observable variables to represent an underlying concept, making it easier for us to understand the data. As in factor analysis, our complex data can be simplified through computer processing, cutting through many variables to discover the underlying concepts or structures.

Overview

Latent class analysis is a technique for simplifying complex data that is used in test construction and validation. It helps determine and verify the underlying concepts or structures—the unobservable latent classes—being measured. LCA attempts to find the underlying structure by looking for ways that cases cluster together rather than looking at correlations. It can help determine the most effective test items and can enhance scoring.

Latent Class Analysis differs from factor analysis in that it approaches the data not by looking at correlations between variables, but by finding the way cases cluster together so that the underlying structure can be identified. Given a sample of cases—research participants, medical patients, objects, etc.—for which we have measures on several variables, we want to know if there is a small number of basic groups into which the cases fall.

When using latent class analysis researchers have the advantage of being able to use categorical data that is either nominal or ordinal. With factor analysis, we assume that we have continuous data measured on an interval scale, that the relationships are linear, and that the data is distributed normally. It can be argued that factor analysis has been used sometimes when these assumptions are not met.

One successful medical application of LCA is the evaluation of diagnostic tests when there is no "gold standard" criterion for evaluating the effectiveness of any of the individual diagnostic tests. LCA can provide estimates of diagnostic accuracy (proportion of correct diagnoses, number of false positives and false negatives, etc.) of the different tests. LCA has been applied in many areas, including marketing research, survey research, sociology, psychology, and education.

Learning Key

Factor analysis: Technique used to simplify complex data. Correlates all items in a scale or correlates many different scales with each other, analyzes the correlations to determine which correlations go together, and seeks the smallest number of factors needed to explain the intercorrelations. A **factor** is a common element in a group of items or scales that go together.

Latent Class Analysis: Technique used to simplify complex data. Finds the underlying structure in data by looking at the way cases cluster together. Can be used with categorical data that is either nominal or ordinal. Even though a **latent class** cannot be directly observed, it is inferred from observed and measured variables and shows underlying connections.

We saw in the last chapter how IRT can aid in item selection during test development and in scoring of the test by computer. LCA can be similarly helpful. The latest revision of the Murphy-Meisgeier Type Indicator for Children® (MMTIC®), a children's personality assessment based on the work of Isabel Myers, used LCA to help determine which items should be included and how they should be weighted to achieve the most effective identification of type preferences. Using LCA with the standardization group data, the test developers identified items that were redundant, as well as items that shared irrelevant associations. As a result, the test was shortened by several items, but the resulting test has greater precision than it had before the items were removed. In addition, when an individual's responses to the instrument are computer-scored, LCA allows for estimating a percentage of accuracy for each of the type dichotomies.

Reliability and Validity

We have said that establishing validity is a complex process, in part because the various aspects of evidence for validity are interrelated. Validity is also complex because it is not a stand-alone measurement concept. Validity is interrelated with reliability and with the appropriate or inappropriate use of a test.

Overview

Reliability is a necessary, but not a sufficient condition for valid measurement. All valid tests are reliable. If a test is not reliable, it cannot be valid, but a reliable test may or may not be valid.

Appropriate use is a key to validity. A test developer can develop a good test, but the validity of that good instrument in actual use in a particular situation depends on a professional who is adequately trained, knows the appropriate use of the instrument, and assures that the results will be used appropriately.

Reliability Necessary for Validity

It is important to note that *reliability is a necessary, but not a sufficient condition for valid measurement*. The reliability of a test limits its potential validity. All valid tests are reliable. No unreliable tests may be valid, but *reliable tests may or may not be valid*.

To illustrate, let's consider again the elastic ruler that we used on page 72 to measure the height of an eight-year-old. With the elastic ruler, height varied considerably with repeated measurement. There was no way each measurement could be correct. We did not have reliability. Therefore, we could not have validity. You'll recall we did better with our steel tape measure. But suppose that while the tape said consistently that our child was 51 inches tall, the child really was 49 inches tall. Our tape measure might be consistent (reliable) but not correct (valid), in this case because the bottom 2 inches of our tape measure were broken off.

The validity of a test can never exceed the reliability of the test. Valid tests not only need to measure what they are designed to measure, but they need to measure it reliably, that is, to do it consistently.

Appropriate Use a Key to Validity

Our discussion to this point has focused on characteristics of tests from the perspective of what a test developer can do to provide a good instrument. Having an instrument that consistently measures a characteristic that relates well to a criterion or other measures of the same construct is great. However, the use of that good instrument in a particular situation is dependent on its appropriate use by a professional

- who is adequately trained,

- who knows that the use of this instrument is appropriate in this situation with these individuals, and

- who can assure that the results will be used in an appropriate manner.

Even a very good instrument can be used inappropriately and in a harmful manner. Even though an instrument may be reliable and valid, its successful use for each individual depends on the skill of the professional who introduces it, answers questions, explains results, and points the person to ways of expanding understanding and usefulness of what is learned. It is the responsibility of the professional to uphold the reliability and validity of the instrument in the context of the test's intended appropriate use.

So, as a professional, you hold the key to validity. Use tests well.

Exercises and Questions to Check Your Understanding

1. **Which are valid statements to make about validity? Mark all that apply.**

   _____ A. Validity can be established with a single study, if the sample is sufficiently large.

   _____ B. Validity is difficult and complicated to establish, involving various methods.

   _____ C. Reliability is more difficult to establish than is validity.

   _____ D. Validity is checking whether the test measures what it intends to measure.

   _____ E. Validity is effected by whether the examiner administers the test appropriately.

   _____ F. If we have validity, we know the test is free of error.

2. **When reliability and validity information are reported in a test manual or in a test review, they are typically reported with what statistic?**

   _____

3. **When we see a table reporting validity information for an instrument, what do we need to do to make the numbers meaningful?**

   _____

4. **Match each of the following with the example that best identifies that particular aspect of validity.**

   a. content-related evidence for validity

   b. criterion-related evidence for validity

   c. construct-related evidence for validity

   d. face validity

   e. factor analysis

   _____ A. Finding a correlation of .85 between a test and an established instrument designed to measure the same thing.

   _____ B. Looking for correlations with other instruments or scales that measure the same or a similar theoretical concept.

   _____ C. Reviewing a quiz or an instrument to determine if the items are all relevant to its purpose and are not too easy or difficult.

_____ D. Using computer analysis to find correlations between items on an instrument for the purpose of seeing groups of items that go together and have a common element.

5. Suppose we have a new Extraversion–Introversion scale and want to establish its validity. We give our new scale and a variety of other established scales to a large group of people. On our new scale, high scores indicate Introversion and low scores Extraversion. Because of this, positive correlations with other scales relate to the Introversion end of the new scale. We obtain the following correlations:

Scale	N	r
Autonomy	47	-.34*
Deference	47	.41**
Intelligence	80	.04
Masculinity–femininity	47	.10
Religiosity	80	.14
Self-confidence	47	-.47***
Self-sufficiency	47	.44**
Sociability	80	-.67***
Suspiciousness	80	.12

A. Think about the meaning of the new scale. Which correlations indicate convergent validity? _____

_____

B. Which correlations indicate discriminant validity? _____

_____

C. Since the correlation with Sociability is so high, would it be possible to use these two scales interchangeably? Why or why not? _____

_____

_____

6. *Mark the best answer.* **Reliability and validity are**

A. related; reliability is required to have validity.

B. interdependent; that is, we need reliability in order to have validity, and we need validity in order to have reliability.

C. independent; reliability and validity have no bearing on each other but must be individually determined.

D. None of the above is true.

7. **Which of the following are reasons why it is important to understand reliability and validity? Mark all that apply.**

_____ A. It helps the test user read articles to keep up-to-date on new developments and research regarding instruments the person uses.

_____ B. It gives a basis to compare similar tests when choosing which one to use.

_____ C. It lets the test user impress clients with the depth of the person's knowledge.

_____ D. It provides a common language to communicate with other professionals in the field about assessments.

_____ E. Ultimately responsibility for the reliability and validity of a particular administration of a psychological test rests with the test user.

_____ F. The insurance company or whoever pays for the test expects it.

6

Norms and Usability

In choosing a good psychological test, considering its reliability and validity will usually be the greatest concerns. However, whether a test has good norms, whether it is user-friendly, and whether it is likely to be helpful in the population where we want to use it can also be crucial. We will consider these factors in this chapter.

Norms

Test norms tell us what the average score is and also how much variability there is among scores. They allow us to compare an individual's score on the test with scores obtained by the standardization group.

Overview

Norms aid interpretation of an individual's test results by providing summary statistics of a standardization group's performance on the test, such as averages and measures of variability. Norms provide a basis for comparison of an individual's results with the performance of a group of other people. Standardization groups need to be large, representative, and well-defined.

Many good tests will have **norms**, which are scores that are used to standardize the test. The scores are gathered by giving the test to defined groups of people, which serve as a basis of comparison for people who will take the test later. A score of 80 on a scale of manual dexterity means nothing unless we have norms to let us know how this particular score compares with the scores of other people. If norms for the manual dexterity test tell us that the mean for large samples of the population is 75 and the SD is 10 for this scale, we can draw some conclusions about our person's skill level. We now know this person's score of 80 is above the mean, at a z-score of +0.5, which is at the 70th percentile, as we can tell from figure 2.8 on page 27.

The interpretation of intellectual ability tests is based on norms. A large standardization sample takes the test, and for each age group, the mean of the standardization group is set as IQ = 100. The percentages in the normal curve that we saw in chapter 2 are used to set the other IQ points for that age group, based on a mean of 100 and a standard deviation of 15.

The standardization group to establish norms for a test should be large, well-defined, and representative of the populations with which the test will be used. Of course, we need to know the demographic characteristics of this standardization group so we can determine whether it is an appropriate comparison group for the individual we are evaluating.

The results of some tests, such as the MBTI instrument, are *not* interpreted in relation to norms. In technical jargon, we'd say the MBTI instrument is not norm-referenced. The objective of the Indicator is to point the respondent to one of the 16 type descriptions. The person's recognition of the fit of the description does not depend on reference to a norm but on his or her judgment about the correct fit.

Sometimes a standardization sample is used for purposes other than providing norms. When we see the term standardization sample, we need to read carefully to interpret the term accurately. For example, Myers' first criterion group for developing the MBTI instrument was a small group of people whose personality types she knew well. She used this group of people to test how well potential items worked. During the 1998 revision process, researchers collected a standardization sample of 3,009 adults, designed to match the U.S. census on age, gender, and ethnicity. This sample was used to test items in the research form, to gather

---

Learning Key

Norms: Summary statistics from scores of a standardization group, used for comparison with an individual's score.

Usability: Practical usefulness of a test.

Base rate: Percentage in the population who have a characteristic or condition of interest.

demographic data for further research, to set the midpoint of each scale, and to estimate the distribution of types in the population. These uses of a standardization sample are important in test construction, but they are not the same as providing norms, which give a reference point for interpretation of results.

Usability

Another characteristic of a good psychological test is usability or practical usefulness. Usability is a broad category and includes a variety of matters such as base rates and user-friendly criteria, including ease of administration and scoring, cost, and availability.

Overview

Usability or practical usefulness is another characteristic of good psychological tests. When we want to identify if a person has a condition or status, the usability of a test may depend on the base rate (frequency of occurrence) of the condition in the population being tested. Tests may not be effective if **base rates** are very high or very low. When a test is used to predict, the relative costs of false positives and false negatives need to be considered in determining cutoff scores, which in turn determine the sensitivity—the accuracy of the cutoff in correctly classifying people—and specificity of the test—accuracy of the cutoff in not classifying people who do not have the condition.

Reliability and validity are essential characteristics, but ease of administration and scoring, reasonable costs, and ready availability are also important. Since efforts to increase usability can sometimes jeopardize reliability, final choice of an instrument often rests on finding the appropriate balance between reliability, validity, and usability.

Base Rates

Whether a test will be useful in actual practice may depend not only on the adequacy of the test itself, but also on the **base rate** of the characteristic in the population where the test is being used. The base rate is the frequency of occurrence of the condition in the population. In the case of a psychological test, it would be the percentage of people in the population who have the characteristic we are testing for. For example, if we were interested in predicting which high school students have ability to do well in college, a group of top students in an elite prep school would have a very high base rate of giftedness, while a class of academically challenged students would have a very low base rate.

Knowing the base rate is important if we want to use a test to make predictions. We might want to use a measurement to predict which students will graduate from medical school. Or we might want to predict which people are good candidates for promotion to a managerial position, or which people are at risk of committing suicide.

If we want to make predictions, and the base rate of the behavior we want to predict is either very high or very low, predictions from a test are less likely to be useful. For example, the Medical College Admission Test (MCAT) is a highly valid test for predicting medical school performance. However, because a high percentage of students who are admitted to medical school actually graduate, even this quite valid test is not likely to help us predict who will graduate if used with students who have already been admitted to medical school. The base rate for graduating is very high. We might have a better prediction rate—percentage of correct predictions— if we predicted that every student admitted to medical school will graduate rather than if we used MCAT scores to predict graduation. On the other hand, if used with college students who are applying for medical school admission, the MCAT works well. The SAT or ACT (American College Test) might not predict very well who will do best in college if we were testing only students at an elite prep school, but these tests are likely to do relatively better in predicting college success among students at a typical high school with a broad range of ability levels.

If we were looking for a measure to predict when people are at risk for committing suicide, we might notice that people who commit suicide tend to have high scores on tests of depression. However, lots of people have high depression scores, but fortunately only a few of them actually commit suicide. The base rate of committing suicide is very low. We will have a much higher percentage of correct predictions in most populations if we say that no one will commit suicide than if we try to use depression scores to predict who is at risk.

Of course, you may say that the cost of a prediction error is much higher if we say someone will not commit suicide when the person actually does, than if we predicted someone was highly suicidal and took appropriate precautions, but the person did not commit suicide. That is true. In chapter 3 we saw the need for balance in weighing the relative risks of a Type I and a Type II error. This need for balance applies here as well. We need to consider the relative costs of *false positives*—saying a person has the condition when they do not—versus *false negatives*—saying a person does not have the condition when in fact they do. As we noted in the first chapter, statistics are not just cut-and-dried sets of facts; we have to use good judgment and common sense in how we apply them.

A test that is used to make an either/or decision like positive or negative diagnosis, or pass or fail, typically has *cutoff scores*. A person receiving a score above the cutoff is classified as having the condition, and a person with a score below the cutoff is classified as not having the condition. Some predictions will be more costly than others, such as predicting a person will not commit suicide, but discovering later that they have. The relative costs are critical in setting a cutoff score.

In your review of tests, you may see the terms *sensitivity* and *specificity*. Sensitivity refers to the accuracy of a cutoff score in identifying people who belong in a particular category. Tests and cutoff scores with good sensitivity have few false negatives. Specificity indicates the accuracy of the cutoff score in excluding those who do not have the condition. Tests and cutoffs with good specificity yield few false positives. If we used a depression scale to predict who is at risk to commit suicide and we set the cutoff at a moderately high level, we would identify most of the potentially suicidal people and have good sensitivity, but we would also identify a large number of people who would not commit suicide—a large number of false positives. If we set the cutoff substantially higher, we would have higher specificity and reduce the number of false positives, but we would also miss more suicidal people and have both more false negatives and lower sensitivity.

Base rates, and sensitivity and specificity, are important considerations in choosing a test if we are planning to use the test to make predictions. If the base rate is either very high or very low in the population where we want to use the test, even a test that has very good reliability and validity in a diverse population may not perform satisfactorily. We may find that using a test in the high or low base rate circumstance will not be helpful. We will then use other methods to try to accomplish our task. For example, if our concern is suicide prevention, we will use careful interviewing and observation to identify when special precautions are needed; just using a test is unlikely to help our prediction of who needs special care.

Fortunately, base rates tend not to be very high or very low in most populations in which we are likely to want to use tests, so base rates will not hinder us from using tests effectively. However, thinking about what the base rate might be is a good thing to do when we are considering whether a test will be useful in a particular situation.

User-friendliness

In choosing a test, we definitely want one that has good reliability and validity, but we also want it to be user-friendly. There are a variety of usability factors to look for, including these:

- A well-written manual that describes clearly the procedure for administration, scoring, and interpretation.

- Ready availability from a reputable publisher who subscribes to the industry-standard *Standards for Educational and Psychological Testing* published jointly by the American Educational Research Association, American Psychological Association, and National Council on Measurement in Education.

- Availability of both online and paper-and-pencil administration formats. Online administration tends to be well accepted and efficient, and often offers scoring options not otherwise available. However, online administration may come at a higher monetary cost than paper-and-pencil administration unless one administers large numbers of tests. (As technology evolves, this may change.)

- A reasonable time requirement. In general, longer tests have higher reliability, but they also increase time expenditure of tester and test taker, and increase the possibility of boredom and lack of cooperation.

In choosing instruments to use, there are advantages to instruments which have wide applicability rather than a narrow focus that makes their use infrequent. Just as we tend to prefer having medical procedures done for us by practitioners who do the procedure regularly and frequently, having instruments we use often makes us more proficient and more knowledgeable than we would be if we used an instrument rarely. Thus, we may find it advantageous to use instruments that can have more than a single purpose. Tests differ in their level of complexity and the amount of expertise required for their use.

There are three levels of psychological and educational tests, A, B, and C. Level A tests are available without restrictions, and there are no special qualifications required for their use. Level B tests require completion of a course in tests and measurement, and Level C tests require the purchaser to have an advanced degree in an appropriate profession, membership in an appropriate professional association, or licensure in an appropriate profession. Finding a test that matches the level of available expertise can be important.

Short forms of tests are sometimes developed for quicker administration, but the shorter length often results in lower reliability. How critical the results are, and how they will be used, will help the user decide whether the time savings are justified.

In selecting tests, one of the best sources for information on commercially available tests is the *Mental Measurement Yearbook* series of the Buros Institute of Mental Measurements, available in major university libraries or online. Each Buros review typically includes usability factors, as well as reliability and validity data. Test publishers who subscribe to the *Standards for Educational and Psychological Testing* provide in either the test manual or supplementary materials much of the information a potential user needs to evaluate whether a test will fit a particular purpose, though the publisher's materials may emphasize the positive factors. You may need to "read between the lines" to determine if there are negative factors that are likely to impact your use of the test in your particular situation.

Sometimes you may be willing to compromise some on the degree of reliability and validity if usability is considerably greater. In the final selection of a test, a balance between usability and reliability and validity is important.

Exercises and Questions to Check Your Understanding

1. **Some psychological tests are norm referenced. Others, such as the MBTI instrument, are not norm referenced. For each statement below, mark yes if the test is norm referenced and no if the test is not norm referenced.**

   _____ A. The test developer gives the test to a standardization group whose scores provide a basis for comparison with people who take the test later.

   _____ B. The test developer gives test items to a standardization sample to determine how well potential items are likely to work.

   _____ C. The test developer gives the test to a standardization group to gather demographic data for use in further research.

   _____ D. The test developer gives the test to a standardization sample to determine the mean and standard deviation of the test.

2. **Use the following terms to fill in the blank in the statements below.** *(Note: Not all possible terms are used.)*

base rate	cutoff score
false negative	false positive
practical usefulness	sensitivity
specificity	

   A. The frequency with which a characteristic or condition occurs in a population is the _____ .

   B. Base rates may impact a test's _____ in a population.

C. When a test is used to predict the presence or absence of a condition, saying a person has the condition when they in fact they do not have the condition makes that prediction a _____ .

D. When a test is used to predict the presence or absence of a condition, the point on the scale at which the person is determined to have the condition (but not to have the condition if they fall below that point) is called the _____ .

E. Tests that have good accuracy in helping us identify only people who have the condition of concern give few _____ results and are said to have good _____ .

P A R T

3

Reading Research Critically

Congratulations! Now that you have traveled this far toward understanding statistics and measurement, you are on your way to critically reading journal articles without feeling intimidated by all the statistical information and jargon. While we may prefer good summaries, it is important that professionals are able to go directly to original sources to get information relevant to their work.

A typical journal article has five main parts:
- Abstract
- Introduction
- Method
- Results
- Discussion

Chapter 7 addresses issues in evaluating the introduction. Chapter 8 addresses the method section, which is packed with details critical to understanding the findings. Chapter 9 considers the reported results, their interpretation, and the summary (abstract) of the study. In each chapter, we will consider questions we can raise about articles we are critiquing.

Reading journal articles is a skill worth having even if it is hard work—and reading them well is hard work.

7

Reading the Introduction

If given the choice, most of us would prefer to get information we need from a known and trusted source in as condensed and simplified a form as possible. We prefer not to have to dig for information in its original raw form and evaluate its adequacy and meaning as we go.

While we may prefer good summaries, it is important that professionals be able to go directly to original sources, usually journal articles, to get information that is relevant to their practice, such as finding a good assessment tool or an effective intervention technique. While many people shy away from journal articles because they are intimidated by all of the statistical information that such articles contain, your newfound knowledge about statistics should help you read journal articles with more confidence.

When we talk about reading research critically, some may think we are being negative, confusing critical and critiquing with criticism. The purpose of critiquing research is not to criticize but to judge the strengths as well as the weaknesses of a study, in hope of understanding what conclusions can be made realistically about a study. We are inclined to assume when something is printed, it must be good. Many respected journals minimize poor quality reports by the peer review process, in which experts who are knowledgeable about the area of research but who are blind as to the study's authorship critically review the article before the journal agrees to publish it. However, even in the best journals, some published articles still contain serious flaws that limit or modify what we can conclude from the study or how we can appropriately use the information. We are wise to critically read journal articles related to our interests and profession for ourselves.

As we begin, it is important to note that no study is perfect. The questions raised in chapters 7, 8, and 9 relate to the ideal study. Just because an article does not meet all the criteria for an ideal article outlined here does not mean it has no value. However, knowing what is ideal helps one evaluate what may be "good enough."

The abstract is at the beginning of an article, but it is a summary and *conceptually* comes at the end of the article. For this reason, we cannot evaluate the abstract until we understand the whole article, so we will look at the abstract last.

In this chapter we will consider ways to critically read the **introduction** of an article. While journal articles are not intended to be works of art, there is no reason for an article to be written in a dull and uninteresting fashion. We can hope the introduction is written well enough that it will catch our interest and set the stage for the presentation of the research. The introduction has three parts:

- presenting the problem;
- reviewing the background literature; and
- stating the purpose, rationale, and hypotheses.

In addition, the author should provide in the introduction a definition of any terms that may be new to most readers, used in different ways than are common, or used in a specific or restricted way. As we consider and critique the introduction to an article, we will address the following questions:

- What is the research question?
- Is it clear how this study (a) relates to and (b) attempts to improve on previous research?
- What are the hypotheses?
- Do the hypotheses address the research question?
- Does the author use a theory to guide the research question and hypotheses?
- Does the author make a convincing argument for the importance of the study?

Presenting the Problem

The **introduction** is the first section following the title and abstract and serves as the beginning for the text of the paper. The title Introduction is rarely used. Most introduction sections begin with a brief description of the research problem or the purpose of the study. As we critically read the introduction to the problem, we want to be able to clearly identify the research question.

Overview

The first one or two paragraphs of a journal article broadly describe the point of the study or the **research problem**. An overview of the **research question**, hypotheses, experimental design, and theoretical implications of the research may be included.

To understand an article and evaluate it, we need to know the purpose of the research. What did the researcher intend to study? The beginning of the introduction announces the topic of the article by presenting the problem the study is about. As we read this announcement, we want to keep in mind a basic question.

What is the research question?

Introductions often begin with a statement of purpose that tells us *why* the study was conducted. For example, the purpose of a study might be helping students learn statistics without fear, a fairly general purpose.

In contrast to the purpose, the **research question** tells us *what* was studied. Some studies give a **problem statement** rather than a research question, but in either case, what we are looking for is a concise sentence that tells us the population, the major variables being studied, and how they are to be tested. Having this statement of the problem in the form of a question is generally seen as preferable because questions demand answers, and systematically trying to find answers to questions is what research is all about.

Using our same example, the research question might be, "Do statistics students show less anxiety as measured by the Manifest Anxiety Scale when instruction has been supplemented with progressive relaxation training?" The question is specific as to population (statistics students), variables to be studied (anxiety measured by the MAS), and how they are to be studied (supplementing instruction with relaxation training).

Unfortunately, not all articles clearly state the purpose of the study and the research question, and often the research questions stated do not contain all the elements we have suggested as desirable. Sometimes the reader needs to infer the question or purpose from other information provided in the article. Sometimes a study will have more than one research question.

Background Literature

As we read the literature review part of the study, we can ask how clearly the author shows the relationship between the current study and previous research, and how the current study attempts to improve on what has been done previously. We will want to ask, Is it clear how the study (a) relates to and (b) attempts to improve on previous research?

Overview

The literature review section summarizes previous research on the topic, highlights one or more questions arising from previous studies, and lays a foundation for showing how the current study adds to previous knowledge on the topic. Thus the literature review informs the reader about the overall problem being investigated and provides the basis for rationales for the specific hypotheses to be studied.

The background literature, usually the longest part of the introduction, can be intimidating. However, once you have a general idea about the main points of the study from reading the abstract and the first section of the introduction, reading the background literature and tying the main points of the past studies to the current study's main points should be easier. Really good writers make this easy by giving enough information to understand previous studies, then relating it to their current research. Incidentally, even though we won't critique the abstract until we understand the whole article, it is still useful to read the abstract to help us get oriented to the paper's main points.

Is it clear how the study (a) relates to and (b) attempts to improve on previous research?

If you are not already familiar with the literature on the topic of a research study, you won't know whether the author has included some of the classic sources as well as the most recent sources. On the other hand, there are some things you can tell about a literature review, even when you are not familiar with the content area.

Learning Key

Introduction: Beginning text of a research article; usually includes presentation of the research problem, a literature review, and statements of the purpose, rationale, and hypotheses of the study.

Research question or problem: Statement of the question or problem the study is trying to answer.

Hypothesis: Statement of a predicted relationship between variables.

Here are some points to consider when critiquing a literature review.

- The review should be comprehensive. We generally expect to find both classic and recent literature covered. If you know a topic has been studied for awhile, you'll expect some older references. However, if all of the studies cited are more than five to ten years old, you can wonder if the recent literature has been covered, or why no one else has been interested in the topic in the last decade.

- It is preferable that the author cite primary sources—the original research studies—rather than review articles or books that describe the study, even though that may be where an author originally learned about the primary source.

- Literature reviews usually contain paraphrases rather than direct quotes from earlier studies. A paraphrase generally takes fewer words, and in paraphrasing one can put all the studies reviewed in the same frame of reference, and when more than one study makes the same point, the author can state the point and cite all the studies that support it in one place without having to repeat the point. So paraphrasing is both economical and makes the literature review more readable.

- It is expected that the author will critically evaluate past studies, making clear their relevance to the present study.

- When there is literature on both sides of a question, both sides should be presented.

These points help us achieve what we are really after—understanding how the present study relates to previous studies and how this study intends to improve on what has already been done. Ideally an author will spell out this latter point quite clearly, but that doesn't always happen.

Of course, a good literature review could also point to the possibility that another study is not needed. For example, if the hypothesis for a study were that "rats will press on a bar faster and longer if they are given a food reward each time than if they are given no reward," it will be obvious from a good literature review that the hypothesis is not new, and that such a study would not likely add anything to the literature on learning and reinforcement, because that hypothesis has been tested many times before. The background literature section should prevent researchers from "reinventing the wheel." Similarly, if a researcher makes a bold claim such as "women are genetically superior to men" and provides no background literature to support such a hypothesis, then the reader may be suspicious and wonder if the study is unscientific.

127

Purpose, Rationale, and Hypotheses

As we read the subpart of the article that gives the purpose, rationale, and hypotheses, we can ask the following:

- What are the hypotheses?

- Do the hypotheses address the research question?

- Does the author use a theory to guide the research question and hypotheses?

- Does the author make a convincing argument for the importance of the study?

Overview

The literature review section should naturally lead to the final subpart of the introduction, which includes a formal statement of the study's research question or purpose, the rationale for that question or purpose, and the specific **hypothesis** or hypotheses to be tested. It should be clear what is being tested and why. There should not be any surprise hypotheses that were not addressed under the background literature subpart. Each hypothesis should have a clear rationale describing the logic behind the predictions.

Although the introduction begins with a subpart that introduces the problem by briefly telling the purpose of the study and stating the research question or problem, the final subpart of the introduction formalizes these statements. It gives the purpose, rationale, and hypotheses. It builds on the initial presentation of the problem and on the literature review to make clear what is being studied and why.

What are the hypotheses?

Hypotheses are intelligent guesses that help researchers seek solutions to problems. A **hypothesis** is a statement of the predicted relationship between two or more variables. A given research study can have one or more hypotheses, as many as are needed to test all aspects of the problem.

Nieswiadomy (1988) introduces hypotheses by suggesting you imagine you are baking a cake; you notice thirty minutes after putting it in the oven that the cake is not rising. You would start thinking of possible reasons. Is the oven turned on? You feel the oven door and it is appropriately warm. Is the temperature not set correctly? You check and it is correctly set at 350 degrees. Did you leave out some ingredient? Then you spot the unopened can of baking soda. Aha! The reason for the flat cake is now apparent. The hunches you had about the reason for the flat cake could be considered hypotheses. After the facts were gathered, you knew your last hypothesis was correct.

Sometimes hypotheses are specifically spelled out as such, while at other times, they may be listed as *predictions* or "We believe such and such will happen." A good hypothesis will be written in a declarative sentence, in the present tense. It will contain the population and variables and reflect the research question or problem statement; and it will be empirically testable. For example, earlier we raised this research question: "Do statistics students show less anxiety as measured by the Manifest Anxiety Scale when instruction has been supplemented with progressive relaxation training?" A hypothesis for this question might be: "Counseling graduate students receiving progressive relaxation training prior to and during statistics training will show significantly less anxiety as measured by the MAS during the final examination, as compared with similar students who do not receive relaxation training."

Do the hypotheses address the research question?

While the research question presents the question to be answered by the study, the hypotheses present possible answers. We will expect that the hypotheses address the research question in a way that they could provide possible answers to the question. We also will expect to find some explanation of how the hypotheses were derived. Hypotheses are not shots in the dark. A source or rationale needs to be stated for each hypothesis. A researcher doesn't merely create a hypothesis and test it, but provides a rationale or case for why that hypothesis should be tested.

The background literature often sets the stage for the rationale. In the literature review before stating our example hypothesis about graduate students and statistics anxiety, we could have cited studies about test anxiety, progressive relaxation in anxiety treatment, and use of the MAS as a measure of anxiety, all of which would show that our hypothesis draws on other scientific findings.

We will want to see that the hypotheses are reasonable and that they are consistent with the research question. While the research question may be somewhat general, we will expect the hypotheses to be quite specific, so we will know whether or not they have been supported or refuted after the data are gathered and analyzed.

Does the author use a theory to guide the research questions and hypotheses?

Generally speaking, a study is more valuable if it tests a theory rather than testing an idea without a theoretical base. We are looking for a connection between some theory of behavior and what the study sets out to do. The term *theory* in science means something much different than the same term in general usage, where it is often regarded as little more than a hunch. In science, a theory is more complex, usually representing several general principles and the connections between them. Theories usually are the result of many studies by many authors.

If a study's research question and hypotheses are not guided by a theory, there is a risk the results will wind up in the "Center for Isolated and Homeless Facts," without any way to relate them to larger bodies of scientific theory. When our hypotheses are based on a theory, we can link them to other research and they are more likely to be linked to other knowledge.

Our proposed study of the effect of relaxation training on statistics anxiety could be related to learning theory or to the body of knowledge supporting cognitive behavioral treatments for anxiety, so it would not wind up as a homeless finding.

Does the author make a convincing argument for the importance of the study?

If the author does a good job spelling out the problem, telling us why it is important, showing what has been done previously and how the present study is going to advance our understanding of the problem, we should be convinced that the study is an important one to do, and that the report of it will be worth our while to read and ponder.

8

Reading the Method Section

Without question, the **method section** of a research article is the most complex. Despite the fact that it often is not very long, it is packed with details that are important for us as we try to understand the study. The purpose of the method section is to provide a detailed description of how the study was conducted. Think of this section as being like a recipe, with a clear description of how to replicate the study. This section is usually divided into subparts, but what subparts are included depends on the nature of the study.

We will consider the method section through three groups of questions that are separated into these categories: sampling method, variables and measures, and research design.

Sampling Method

The first part of the method section in an article typically relates to the sample used and the methodology the researchers used for selecting and assigning the sample. As we read about the sample, we will want to consider these questions:

- Who comprised the sample?
- What type of sampling procedure was utilized?
- What is the likely population to which the authors want to generalize the findings?
- Does the sample appear to be representative of the population and unbiased? In what ways might the sample differ from the population?

- Does attrition occur, and does this bias the sample?
- To what degree do you believe the results of the study can be generalized to the population?
- What procedures are used to assign participants to groups or conditions, and do they seem appropriate?
- Are ethical issues regarding participants discussed?

Overview

The method section in most research articles begins with a participants subpart containing information such as (a) the number of participants, how they were selected, and how they were assigned to groups; (b) major relevant demographic characteristics; (c) description of agreements and payments; and (d) statement of ethical principles used in relation to the participants.

Participants are described in the first part of most method sections. *Participants* is the term most often used when humans are involved in the study while *subjects* is the term most often used when animals are in the study. (If you look in older literature, you will see that human participants always were referred to as subjects.) We will want the sample to be described in terms of major relevant demographic characteristics. We will want a description of agreements and payments made, how the sample was selected, how members were assigned to groups, and how ethical issues were handled. This information will help readers make comparisons of samples across different studies and determine if the results can be generalized.

Who comprised the sample?

The first part of the method section needs to give us a thorough description of the participants in the study, both so we can judge the adequacy of the sample and so interested researchers will be able to replicate the study later using a similar group. The number of participants and demographic characteristics that are relevant to the study need to be included, such as age, sex, marital status, socioeconomic status, level of education, race, and ethnicity. For nonhuman subjects we will expect to find: (a) genus, species; (b) strain number or location of supplier; (c) number, sex, age, weight, and physiological condition; and (d) ethical guidelines on treatment and handling.

As you read the description of the sample, you will be looking for clues about the representativeness of the sample, the equivalence of different groups, and whether participant variables have been properly controlled.

What type of sampling procedure was utilized?

In chapter 3, you were introduced to several types of samples, including probability, or random, samples and nonprobability, or non-random, samples. We will consider them, and a few others, in more detail here.

Most samples, including those described in chapter 3, are **direct samples**, which gather data directly from members of the sample. **Archival samples** use data that have been gathered and recorded, such as vital statistics, census data, medical records, and school records. Archival samples have the advantages of ease of data collection and the minimized risk of having experimenter bias influence participants, because the data are already collected. However, the advantages of archival studies tend to be outweighed by the inability to verify the accuracy of the data or fill in any missing information. There are also selective factors that go into the collection and retention of data. For example, a college alumni office is much more likely to keep track of, and maintain, data on successful graduates than unsuccessful ones, for a variety of reasons. Some information about unsuccessful grads will never be collected, or they may be harder to track, and other information may conveniently be "lost."

Archival studies are sometimes the only reasonable way to answer a research question, or the most cost-effective way to gather information that will help determine the variables for more definitive direct studies. The reader just needs to be aware of the limitations of archival studies and the fact that conclusions will be less definitive, because there is no way to assure the accuracy and completeness of the information. Direct samples are preferred when possible.

Direct samples can be either probability samples or nonprobability samples. Probability samples involve the use of a random selection process in choosing the members of the sample. To sample randomly, we try to see that chance is the only thing that determines who is included in our sample. With a **random sample**, the researcher hopes the variables of interest (whatever we want to study) in the population will be present in the sample in approximately the same proportions as would be found in the whole population, though of course there is no guarantee this will happen. We will consider three kinds of random samples: simple random sampling, stratified random sampling, and systematic random sampling.

In *simple random sampling*, every member of the population has an equal and independent chance of being included in the sample. As we noted in chapter 3, if the population were small, we could put everyone's name on a slip of paper, put the slips in a hat, and have a blindfolded assistant pull out the number of names we need. The more common procedure for achieving a simple random sample is listing and numbering all members of a population, and using a table of random numbers to choose which members of the population will be in the sample.

Because there is no order or sequence in a table of random numbers, there should be no bias in the selection process. Simple random samples are fairly rare, because typically it is not possible to identify every member of the population, something which you must do to assure that every member has an equal chance of being included.

In *stratified random sampling*, the population is divided into subgroups, or strata, based on variables of importance in the study. After the population is divided into strata, a random sample is taken from each of the subgroups. You are familiar with the samples taken by pollsters, in which factors such as gender, socio-economic status, age, and urban vs. rural are taken into account. Since a simple random sample might not include the same proportions of each of these factors as exist in the population, the stratified random sampling process tries to assure the sample is representative in these ways. When polls have been taken over extended periods of time, researchers know what proportions of each factor are needed to have a reasonably representative sample. The stratified random sampling approach works fairly well for pollsters, but for most studies we don't know what the relevant biasing factors are, or we have no way to control them, so this kind of sampling is not common in behavioral research.

Systematic random sampling involves selecting every kth element of the population, such as every seventh or twentieth individual. One first gets a list of the total population, decides how big the sample needs to be, then divides the population size by the size of the sample wanted, to find the k sampling interval. For this to be a truly random process, one must be able to assume the listing of the population is complete and is random with respect to the variable of interest. For example, if the population listing was an alphabetical listing of names, and ethnicity was relevant to the study, the fact that some ethnic groups have large numbers of names beginning with the same letter might make this a problematic selection scheme. One also must randomly decide where to start, that is, which member of the population is the first to be chosen. We might be looking for every seventh person on the list, but we would want to randomly and independently decide which person to start with using a table of random numbers, say the 29th person, and then take every seventh person from then on, picking up at the beginning after getting to the end of the population list.

While many people assume most samples in the behavioral sciences are random, that is not true. Random samples are critical when we want to apply the findings directly, such as in conducting a poll to predict the outcome of an election. Most behavioral science research is not designed to be applied directly, but rather to test theories and explore general principles. In this kind of research, the findings will not stand on their own but will be combined with other studies using a variety of methods and participants to see what findings converge.

The principle of **convergence** tells us that no one experiment provides the final answer, but each experiment helps us rule out alternate explanations and aids in the process of zeroing in on the truth. Each experiment has flaws. When a wide range of experiments have been done, with the different experiments using different techniques and approaches, and each being flawed in different ways, and yet the evidence all points in the same direction, we have *converging evidence*. No single experiment is perfect, but the evidence from many studies can lead us to strong conclusions. Because most studies are only seeking to be part of this kind of web of evidence, the frequent use of nonprobability samples in the behavioral sciences is not a major issue.

In *nonprobability sampling*, the sample is chosen by nonrandom methods. Typically nonprobability samples are chosen because they are more convenient and they allow us to use participants who are available and are willing to volunteer.

Samples of convenience are the most common form of a nonprobability sample. The researcher chooses readily available participants for the study, such as students in an introductory psychology class. This kind of sampling is least expensive in terms of time and money, but there is no way to judge the representativeness of the sample.

A variation on convenience sampling is the *snowball sample* in which the researcher uses early participants to help recruit other potential participants. This kind of networking can be particularly useful when people may be reluctant to make themselves known, such as in a study of substance abusers. However, snowball samples may suffer from inbreeding—the sample may be more narrow and homogeneous than desired—or from contamination as participants talk with each other about the research.

Learning Key

Method section: Detailed description of participants and how the study was conducted.

Direct sample: Gathering data directly from members of the sample.

Archival sample: Using data that have already been gathered and recorded (vital statistics, medical or school records).

Random sample: Only chance determines which members of a population are selected to be in a sample. In a simple random sample, every member of the population has an equal and independent chance of being included.

Sample of convenience: Readily available participants chosen for a study (students in a psychology class).

Convergence: Principle that while no one experiment provides a final answer, evidence from a wide range of experiments points in the same direction.

Self-selected samples are people who respond to open invitations to call in or send in their responses. It is unclear who such a sample represents. *Haphazard samples* are recruited in public places where people may have time on their hands, such as in malls or airports. Self-selected and haphazard samples are difficult to replicate and run the danger of being biased.

Nonprobability systematic samples involve a systematic but nonrandom process for sample selection, like taking the first fifty people who walk through the door at a convention. While some researchers describe these samples as random, we can suspect that early birds may be systematically different from latecomers, so this kind of sample is *not* random.

What is the likely population to which the authors want to generalize the findings?

Sometimes researchers will state specifically what population the sample was drawn from and to which the results of the study will be generalized. Many times you will have to determine for yourself to whom the researcher intends to generalize the results because it has not been stated. In any case, be aware that often the researcher wants to generalize to a broader population than is accessible to be sampled. Sometimes the group we want to generalize to is called the *target population*, while the population available to be sampled from is called the *accessible population*. If we were interested in studying schizophrenia, for example, all persons with schizophrenia would be the target population, but obviously the accessible population does not include all the people with schizophrenia in the world, because we have no way of sampling all of them. We will study people with schizophrenia who are accessible.

Does the sample appear to be representative of the population and unbiased? In what ways might the sample differ from the population?

Our goal in drawing a sample is to have it be as representative of the population as possible. However, even a carefully drawn random sample will not be perfectly representative of the population from which it is drawn. Whenever we draw a sample from a population, there will be *sampling error*. Sampling error is the difference between the measurements we get from a sample as compared to the measurements we would get if we were able to measure every individual in the population.

Sampling bias, on the other hand, occurs when samples are not carefully selected. For example, if we were drawing names out of a hat in choosing a sample, there would be bias if everyone did not have an equal chance of being drawn because some of the names were written on different sizes or different thicknesses of paper than the others, and thus were more likely to be drawn.

A famous example of sampling bias occurred in 1936 when *Literary Digest* surveyed 2.5 million eligible voters to see if they planned to vote for Alf Landon, the Republican, or Franklin D. Roosevelt, the Democrat, for president. Based on their survey, the *Digest* predicted Landon would win by a landslide. As you recall from American history, it was Roosevelt who won by a landslide. What went wrong? It was a case of sampling bias. Participants in the survey were drawn from telephone books and automobile registration lists. In the depressed economy of 1936, members of the Republican Party were more likely to have telephones and automobiles.

Even random sampling procedures are subject to bias if some of the people selected for the sample do not agree to be in the study. We can send a questionnaire to a random sample of a population, but if some people do not fill it out and return it, we may not have a representative sample if there are systematic differences between those who respond and those who do not.

There is no simple way to know if a sample is representative and unbiased, and we can rarely be certain on this one. You will want to use your best judgment, given the information provided. You will want to know if there are particular ways in which this sample may differ from the population the researcher believes it is drawn from.

Some possible variables that may make a sample unrepresentative of the population are raised in the following questions:

- Does the fact that these people volunteered to be in the sample make a big difference, such as if they were required to admit to some deviant behavior?

- Was the sample self-selected, and could that make a difference? Self-selected participants are responding to an open invitation to be in a study, rather than just agreeing to be in the study after the experimenter selected them.

- Were participants required to endure physical or psychological discomfort or risk?

- Do we have any idea how many nonvolunteers turned down the request to be in the research?

- Are there demographic characteristics of the sample that appear quite unlike the population?

Does attrition occur? And does this bias the sample?
If participants drop out during the course of the study, a researcher has an obligation to point out this attrition to the reader, though it does not always get reported.

Sometimes the reader will discover there was attrition by noting a difference between the original N in a group and the N reported in the results section. If there is attrition, you will need to make a judgment about whether those dropping out may have biased the sample. The sample would be biased if the people who dropped out were systematically different from those who remained in the study.

To what degree can the results of the study be generalized to the population?

Combining your understanding of the way the sample was drawn, the nature of the population, your overall impression of the representativeness of the sample, and possible biasing factors, you need to make a judgment about how appropriately the author will be able to generalize the findings of the study to the intended population. While you may be inclined to reserve judgment until you see how the author handles these issues in the discussion section, it is well if you make a mental note now of limitations on generalizability that you see.

What procedures are used to assign participants to groups or conditions? And do they seem appropriate?

Once a sample has been *selected*, we need to see how members of the sample are *assigned* to the different treatment groups or conditions. Ideally, a randomization procedure will be used. Even if the sample was not randomly selected, random assignment to conditions is still possible, and doing so will help minimize problems related to the selection process. If any assignment procedure other than a random procedure is used, the researcher should reassure you that the groups were equivalent before the experiment started. Random assignment of participants to the different groups in a study is necessary for a study to have a true experimental design, as we will see later in our discussion of research designs.

Are ethical issues regarding participants discussed?

Typically very little space in a research article is given to discussion of ethical issues. Most articles contain only a sentence or two stating that participants' rights were protected and informed consent was obtained. This may not be a major concern, since most articles probably do represent work with no ethical flaws because at most universities and colleges, where much research is done, researchers must seek the approval of the Institutional Review Board (IRB) which has critical oversight for studies with human participants. (There is also a review board for animals, the Institutional Animal Care and Use Committee (IACUC.) Questions you can have in mind surrounding ethical treatment of participants include the following:

• Was informed consent obtained?

- Is there information about provisions for anonymity or confidentiality?

- Were any vulnerable participants used, such as institutionalized persons or mentally handicapped individuals?

- Does it appear participants might have been coerced in any way to participate?

- Do the benefits to the participants of participation in the study outweigh the risks?

- Were participants provided the opportunity to ask questions about the study or told how they could get the results of the study?

Variables and Measures

We are now ready to look at the independent and dependent variables and the measurement instruments used in the study. As we read this section, we will want to consider these questions:

- What is the independent variable in the study and how is it operationally defined?

- Are levels of the independent variable appropriate?

- What is the dependent variable in the study and how is it operationally defined?

- What reliability and validity evidence is presented for the measures used in the study? Are scoring, rating, or judging procedures, if used, reliable and valid?

- What are some possible confounding variables that may influence the results of the study? To what degree are you confident that alternative explanations have been ruled out?

 Overview

Many research articles have a method subpart relating to variables and measures used in the study. Variables of interest are the **independent** (cause) **variable** that is manipulated or controlled by the experimenter, the **dependent** (effect or outcome) **variable** that is influenced by the experimenter's control of the independent variable, and **confounding variables** that are extraneous, uncontrolled variables that may effect or create results. We obtain information from the research article about the variables by looking for **operational definitions**, which are publicly observable ways to measure or control variables. Measures are the instruments, materials, experimental equipment, or judges used to gather and code data about the variables. We look for evidence of reliability and validity for these measures, including the **study validity**—or appropriateness for this situation—of the measures. We are looking for both **internal validity** and **external validity** of the study, whether changes in the dependent variable are really due to the independent variable, and whether the results can be generalized to other groups and situations.

Just as a recipe for cookies needs ingredients, one or more subparts of the method section will describe the instruments or measures used in the study. We will want to identify the independent and dependent variables, which may be described in the method section, if they were not included in the introduction. We want to know about the instruments, materials, apparatus, or judges used to gather and code data. Judges are trained observers who rate participants' behavior by some objective method during the experiment or determine whether a behavior does or does not meet certain criteria. We want to find operational definitions for the independent and dependent variables, and we want to consider possible confounding variables that may be threats to the internal and external validity of the study. We want to see if all physical aspects of the study are described so others can replicate the study if desired.

Learning Key

Independent variable: Cause or influencing variable that is manipulated or controlled by the experimenter.

Dependent variable: Effect or outcome variable; what is influenced by the experimenter's manipulation or control of the independent variable.

Operational definition: A concrete, publicly observable way to measure a variable in a study.

Confounding variable: Variable the researcher does not control but that may create results or be a competing explanation for results.

Study validity: Validity of a particular measure with these participants, for this specific purpose, in this specific study.

Internal validity: Degree to which changes in the independent variable do influence the dependent variable in the way suggested by the results of a study.

External validity: Degree to which the relationship between the independent and dependent variables in a study applies to other people, times, and settings; degree to which results of a study can be generalized.

What is the independent variable and how is it operationally defined?

The **independent variable** is the *cause* variable, the variable that is thought to influence the dependent (or *effect* or *outcome*) variable. In an experiment, the independent variable is the variable that is manipulated by the experimenter. It is the treatment, procedure, condition, or status that causes or leads to a consequence or outcome that is dependent on it. Don't take the word *manipulate* too literally. An experimenter may simply compare two pre-existing groups without manipulating anything in the puppet-on-a-string sense. The independent or experimental variable is the one the researcher controls, as in what treatments or conditions are provided and who gets which treatments, assuming people agree to participate.

The **operational definition** tells us how the independent variable will be measured or observed in this study. An operational definition is a publicly observable way to measure or manipulate a variable. Sometimes the operational definition is provided by specific research instruments that are used to gather the data. For example, if levels of depression were the independent variable, scores on the Beck Depression Inventory might operationally define what was meant by depression in this study. Operational definitions are especially important in the behavioral sciences because so many of the terms used in research are also used in everyday language and are terms about which people already have pre-existing biases. Operational definitions help make clear what is really being measured and studied, not what lay people may think the terms mean.

The researcher needs to provide an explanation and operational definition of the independent variable so the reader can understand it and try to determine if the experiment is *really* doing what the researcher claims it is doing. Is it reasonable to assume that what is described is really measuring what the experimenter thinks it is measuring? Don't be thrown off by big words the researcher uses. Sometimes the author will specifically state how a variable is being operationally defined; other times you have to determine what the operational definition is by looking at the procedures used to measure the variable.

Note if any kind of validity check for the independent variable is included. If the study is about stress, the description may suggest the manipulation could be stressful, but did the participants actually find it stressful? Is any evidence provided (such as physiological measures or post-experiment questionnaires to determine what kinds of stress levels were achieved) that confirms the validity of what the experimenter did? (Did the participants really find the experimental condition stressful?) Since ethical concerns don't allow extremes and instead require researchers to reduce or temper their manipulations, some kind of evidence that the manipulation really had the intended purpose may be important.

Are levels of the independent variable appropriate?

One of the early decisions a researcher must make is whether the independent variable will have multiple levels, and whether any levels will be continuous or categorical. Does the independent variable have a continuous range of values, like IQ scores do, or is it dichotomous (either-or) like gender? If there is a range of values, are we able to reliably measure them, or will it make more sense to treat them as a series of categories, like age (treating people as groups, such as 20–29, 30–39, 40–49, etc.)? Determining whether there will be levels of the independent variable occurs at the point of formulating the hypotheses. If a hypothesis is stated in categorical terms (like men will score higher than women), the independent variable should be defined in categorical terms. If the hypothesis is stated as a relationship that varies across the range of possible scores (like age will be negatively correlated with performance), then it would not be appropriate for the independent variable to be broken into dichotomous or nominal categories. We are looking for two things here:

- consistency between the hypothesis and the operational definition of the independent variable, and

- whether that operational definition is reasonable given what we know about the nature of the variable.

Setting levels of the independent variable often is not a simple matter. Consider the hypothesis, "Younger people learn new things more easily than older people." The age groupings the researcher chooses to represent younger and older people will be crucial to the study. There are several options.

- The researcher could choose extreme groups, like a group 20 and younger to represent younger people and a group 80 and older to represent older people. This might maximize the effect, if there is one, but it would minimize the amount of information we would learn about the relationship of age and learning.

- The researcher could choose a continuous range of age categories, like 20–39, 40–59, 60–79, and 80–99. Alternatively a discontinuous range could include categories like these: 20–25, 40–45, 60–65, and 80–85. Both continuous and discontinuous ranges can be appropriate, depending on what is being studied, though they give us different information about the variable. In our example, neither of these sets of ranges directly gets at our hypothesis, since our hypothesis related only to younger and older people and predicted nothing about the people that are in-between. However, if our hypothesis predicted a progressive decline over the age span, then the intermediate levels would be needed.

- The researcher also could do a median split, by ranking all the members of the sample by age and dividing at the median. While this would give us groups that are younger and older, there are problems with this frequently used approach. Falling above or below the median in the sample does not necessarily place a person in a category consistent with the theory being tested. Being 45.8 or more years old does not necessarily mean one is older as usually defined.

If an extreme-groups process is used, the potential for significant experimental effects is maximized. However, we may see the generality of the findings reduced. For example, if we are studying the effects of stress and our stress condition is taking people up in an airplane for a first-time parachute jump and telling them on the way up that their parachute was packed by a new trainee who had only thirty minutes of training in how to pack parachutes, we are likely to see some stress effects!

On the other hand, that kind of stress condition may be too extreme to relate meaningfully to the more typical kinds of stress people face. Using a stressful condition that was closer to normal experience might be more meaningful. Also, note that we would have a hard time justifying that the benefits to our participants outweigh the risks; such an experimental condition would not pass ethical muster. The important point here is that examining the levels of the independent variable gives the reader an idea about whether they match the hypothesis and whether the choice was meaningful and appropriate. Common sense is as important here as research expertise.

What is the dependent variable and how is it operationally defined?

The **dependent variable** is the *effect* or *outcome* variable, the one that is influenced by the experimenter's manipulation or control of the independent variable. In the parachute example above, the independent variable would be whether or not the jumper was given the story about the inexperienced parachute packer, and the dependent variable would be whatever measures we were taking of anxiety, perhaps a questionnaire, physiological indicators of stress, or continued willingness to jump. The dependent variable must be

- clearly defined,
- valid, and
- stated in advance.

While a researcher is always interested in what other outcomes besides those hypothesized might result from the manipulation of the independent variable, any results not predicted in advance can only be used in possible hypotheses for future research, not as findings of the current study. The reason for this is that these unpredicted findings might just be chance occurrences, and to report and treat them as findings would increase the risk of a Type I error—saying something is significant when it really is only a chance finding.

The research instruments or measures that are being used to gather the data typically provide the operational definition of the dependent variable. These may be counts of observable physical or psychological events. Stress effects would not be defined abstractly, but clearly spelled out so we know what the author is looking for, such as changes in physiological measures, anxious statements, or refusal to sky-jump again.

The operational definition of a dependent variable may be a standardized psychological test, a behavioral rating scale, or perhaps a tailor-made instrument when no established instrument is available to do the job. When an established measure is used, such as the Beck Depression Inventory, relatively little explanation or description is needed. When a generally unknown measure or a tailor-made measure is used, a thorough description and explanation of its applicability are needed.

What reliability and validity evidence is presented for the measures used in the study? Are scoring, rating, or judging procedures, if used, reliable and valid?

As we evaluate the operationalized independent and dependent variables, the evidence for the reliability and validity of the measures used is important. When the measures are well established, like the Stanford-Binet, the Beck, or the MMPI, statements about reliability and validity are not required, since it is assumed a reader who is not familiar with those instruments can look them up in reference materials. However, when the measures are not well established, and especially when they are contrived or tailor-made for the study, it is essential that reliability and validity information is given.

Chapters 4 and 5 described reliability and validity. We will want to be sure that the types of reliability and the validity evidence given by the author are appropriate for the measures as they are used in the study. For example, test-retest reliability is appropriate when we can assume the characteristic being measured is stable over time, and criterion-related validity is possible when a *gold standard* for that characteristic already exists.

In addition to the usual considerations about construct-, content-, and criterion-related validity evidence, we also need to be concerned about what is sometimes called **study validity**. Study validity refers to the validity of this measure when used in this experiment with these participants for this specific purpose. A measure may have excellent validity in general and still not be appropriate for use in this study. A highly valid IQ test may have poor study validity if it is used with people whose primary language is one other than the one the test uses, or a personality test with high construct validity may have low study validity if it is used with people who do not comprehend the vocabulary used because they are young or lack the appropriate educational level.

The act of measuring may also impact the dependent variable. The fact that participants know they are in an experiment and are being observed may effect how they behave. Having people chart how many cigarettes they smoke, or how much food they eat, may well change use or consumption patterns since similar charting has been shown to be an effective treatment technique in helping people gain control of a behavior. In looking at the reliability and validity of the measures used in a study, think about the impact of the measurement process and consider if the measurement process may interfere with the experimental objective, particularly if the impact is greater on one experimental group than on the others.

If the data gathering process includes the making of judgments, as in scoring responses, making ratings, or making judgments about whether or not something occurred, you will want to see some evidence that these procedures are reliable and valid. Inter-rater reliability—having more than one rater rate the same materials and correlating the results—may be reported, or perhaps the experimenter will document the effectiveness of the techniques used in some kind of pilot study. Similarly, if any kind of experimental equipment (such as physiological recording devices, counters, etc.) is used in the study, be looking for evidence of its accuracy and reliability as well.

What are some possible confounding variables that may influence the results of the study? To what degree are you confident that alternative explanations have been ruled out?

Researchers hope to show that the independent variable results in change in the dependent variable, and that the effects can be generalized from the sample to the population. They hope to keep extraneous or **confounding variables** from influencing the results. Confounding variables are ones the researcher does not control, or chooses not to control, that may be creating the results. These confounds, or competing explanations for the results, are threats to internal and external validity.

Internal validity refers to whether the experiment represents what it is intended to represent. It relates to the confidence we can have that changes in the dependent variable really are due to the independent variable, and not to other things. Threats to internal validity are things other than the independent variable that could influence the dependent variable or that might explain the results of the study. Here are some threats to internal validity.

145

- Selection bias. Results are attributed to the independent variable, when in fact they are due to differences in the participants before the independent variable was manipulated. For example, in a study of treatment for stopping smoking, a researcher might recruit a group of smokers who said they wanted to quit, but might use as a control group a similar number of people who had not shown a desire to quit. Differences in motivation of the two groups could account for the study results, not the treatment procedure.

- History. A history threat occurs when some event besides the experimental treatment occurs during the course of the study, and this event effects the dependent variable. For example, a study compared two different types of social support for families of soldiers at two different military bases. During the course of the experiment, the soldiers at one base were deployed overseas. Differences in the responses of the two groups at the end of the experiment could easily be related to the deployment, rather than to differences in support provided.

- Maturation. During the study changes may occur within the participants that influence the results, such as new learning or the maturity that comes with increasing age.

- Testing. Posttest scores may be affected by the fact the participants did the pretest, and perhaps learned their results.

- Mortality. Dropout rates, called mortality, may be different in the experimental and control groups.

External validity concerns the degree to which the results of a study can be generalized. Will these results hold true with other groups in other times and places? Here are some threats to external validity.

- Hawthorne Effect. This occurs when participants respond in a certain manner because they are aware they are being observed. This term comes from a famous study on worker productivity at the Hawthorne plant of Western Electric Company in Illinois. Each time a change was made in working conditions, productivity improved, which eventually lead researchers to the conclusion that the increases in productivity were the result of participants' awareness they were involved in a research study and were being observed. The Hawthorne Effect can affect external validity by making the results not generalizable to other groups who would not be similarly observed. It also can be considered a threat to internal validity, in that being observed is accounting for some of the effects, rather than the effects being due to the independent variable.

- Experimenter effect. This occurs when researcher characteristics or behavior (for example, facial expressions, clothing, age, gender, how questions are asked) influences participant behavior.

- Reactive effects of the pretest. When participants are sensitized to the treatment through taking the pretest, this can affect posttest results. This is similar to the testing internal validity threat. It is different, however, in that in this case the pretest is acting as a catalyst with the independent variable in bringing about the results on the posttest.

We noted in chapter 3 that when we know an experimental result is significant—that it is unlikely to have happened by chance—then it allows us to *generalize* the finding. Here we are saying that we need external validity to be able to generalize a result. This is not a contradiction. We first need statistical significance, or we can't be sure the result wasn't just a chance occurrence. Once we have statistical significance, we still must be concerned about external validity. Are the results such that we can reasonably generalize them to other groups and situations?

Internal and external validity are related. When the researcher attempts to control for internal validity, external validity typically decreases. Making the conditions very circumscribed helps the internal validity, but may make the results less generalizable. On the other hand, when the researcher is concerned with external validity or generalizability, stricter controls may reduce internal validity. Thus the researcher needs to balance both internal and external validity concerns. The experimenter may be more rigorous in one way or another to reduce some of these threats, and if so, you will need to consider how effective these efforts may have been.

We present this discussion of confounding variables here because they compete with the independent and dependent variables as possible explanations for what happened in the study. Be aware, however, that you may get ideas about possible confounding variables in other sections of the paper besides the method section, such as in the results or discussion section.

Research Design

Our final set of questions for the method section of a research article relate to the research design used in the study. We will want to consider the design through these questions:

- Looking back at the original research question, what type of question is being asked? Is the study attempting to determine causality?

• What type of research design is used in the study?

• Is there a control group? If so, how was it obtained?

• Is the design suitable to test the hypotheses and does it answer the research question?

• Are the methods and procedures clearly described in sufficient detail to be understood and replicated?

Overview

As we read a research article, we need to understand the research design used in the study. We are looking for details of the methods and procedures and for the directions of how to do the study if someone were to try to repeat it. We want to know what type of research design was used, whether the design included a **control group**, and if that group was comparable to the **experimental group**.

A cookie recipe not only needs a list of ingredients, but it needs detailed directions. A research article also needs a detailed account of the methods and procedures used in the study. We examine what was done in the study by looking at the research design.

Occasionally an article will have a specific subpart about the research design. Other times the information about research design will be in a *procedure* subpart that also includes information about the variables and measures. Either way, as we read about the research design, we are looking for sufficient detail so that the study could be done again by someone else. Just as we want directions for making cookies to be clear so that we can make the same cookies again, we also want the research design to be described clearly so that the study could be replicated.

Looking back at the original research question, what type of research question is being asked? Is the study attempting to determine causality?
Research studies come in three basic forms, based on the research question being asked: descriptive studies, relational studies, and causal studies.

• Descriptive studies attempt to describe something that is going on. They address questions like "Does x exist?" "What is x like?" "To what extent does x exist?" "What are its characteristics?" A public opinion poll trying to find out the proportion of people who hold various opinions is primarily descriptive in nature.

148

- Relational studies look at the relationship between two or more variables. Relational studies assume you can first describe each variable by measuring and observing it, but the studies are asking, "Is there an association or relationship between x and y?" Often correlation coefficients are used to demonstrate the extent and direction of these relationships. A survey that looked separately at attitudes of men and women on an issue would be relational, in that it would be looking at the relationship between gender and attitudes.

- Causal studies attempt to determine whether one or more variables, such as a program or treatment variable, cause or affect one or more outcome variables. Such studies assume you can describe both the cause and the effect variables and that you can show they are related to each other. They address questions such as "Does x cause, lead to, or prevent changes in y?" "Does x cause more change in y than does z?" "Does x cause more change in y than does z under certain conditions but not under other conditions?" A study to determine the effect of an advertising campaign on changes in proportions of voters planning to vote for one party or the other would be a causal study.

As you look back at the research question presented in the introduction of the article, into which of these three categories does it fit?

- Is it merely looking for the existence of a phenomenon?
- Is it looking at the possible relationship between two or more variables?
- Is it asking if one variable affects the other variable (causality)?

What type of research design is used in the study?

In answering this question, we will focus on some basic distinctions that help us know whether the research design fits the kind of question being asked. These distinctions also help us know later, as we evaluate the results and discussion sections, whether the claims that are made for the study are consistent with the possibilities for the type of design used.

What are the different major types of research designs? Trochim (2001) suggests a useful threefold classification that follows from asking two key questions.

First, does the design use random assignment of participants into groups? If random assignment is used, we can call the design a randomized experiment or true experiment. Note that we are talking about random assignment, not random sampling.

If random assignment is not used, then we have to ask a second question: Does the design use either multiple groups or multiple waves of measurement (measuring on more than one occasion)? If the answer is yes, we would label it a *quasi-experimental design*. If no, we would call it a *non-experimental design*. This threefold classification is graphically displayed in the decision tree in figure 8.1.

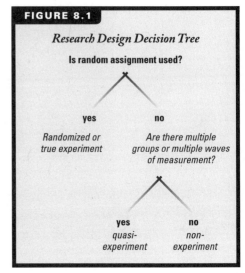

FIGURE 8.1

Research Design Decision Tree

Understanding the research design is especially useful in considering the internal validity of a study. A randomized experiment is likely to have the best internal validity and is also the strongest of the three designs when the researcher wants to establish a cause-effect relationship. A non-experiment is generally the weakest both in terms of internal validity and establishing cause. Quasi-experiments obviously fall in-between.

Let's consider several kinds of research designs. We will use some symbols researchers often use.

- R stands for random assignment of participants to groups.

- N stands for nonequivalent, what we have when participants are not randomly assigned.

- O stands for observation or measurement of the dependent variable.

- X stands for an experimental treatment or intervention.

- Subscripts are used after Xs and Os to indicate first treatment, second treatment, first observation, second observation, and so forth.

The first two designs are randomized true experiments. Each begins with random assignment of participants to conditions, as represented by R. In the first design, we have two groups, both randomly assigned. The first group gets an intervention (X) while the second group gets none. Then both groups get a measurement of the dependent variable (O). For example, we could evaluate a treatment for anxiety by randomly assigning volunteers to either the experimental (treatment) group or the control (no-treatment) group. We give both groups the anxiety test after the experimental group has had treatment to see if the experimental group has lower anxiety levels than the control group.

Posttest Only Randomized Experiment with Control Group

R	X	O	(Experimental group)
R		O	(Control group)

In the second design, we again have two groups, randomly assigned. This time both get a pretest (O_1) before the experimental group gets the intervention. Then both receive the posttest (O_2).

Pretest-Posttest Randomized Experiment with Control Group

R	O_1	X	O_2 (Experimental group)
R	O_1		O_2 (Control group)

In the first design, we are banking on random assignment to result in reasonably equivalent groups—experimental and control. The second design has the advantage of a pretest for both groups which allows us to determine if indeed the two groups perform at equivalent levels prior to the experimental intervention. In both experiments we look for a cause-effect relationship between treatment and anxiety levels.

The next design is a quasi-experiment with a pre-post nonequivalent groups design. We know it's not a true experiment because random assignment is not used. Because we do not control the assignment, the groups may be nonequivalent or not similar to each other. We know it is a quasi-experiment because there are both multiple groups (experimental group and comparison group) and multiple waves of measurement (observations O_1 and O_2). To use our earlier example, we would be taking two already existing groups, giving both the pretest, and then giving the experimental group the treatment, followed by both groups getting the posttest.

Pretest-Posttest Nonequivalent Groups

N	O_1	X	O_2 (Experimental group)
N	O_1		O_2 (Comparison group)

This design would be used when random assignment to groups was not possible. Why might that be? If researchers ran the world, random assignment would be the rule, but researchers do not run the world. Other forces decide who gets which treatment: judges decide who gets which sentence, parents don't allow their children to be subjected to treatments they don't agree with, and employers don't want a researcher deciding who gets what training. However, even without random assignment, the pretest measure in this design would allow comparison of the two groups' performance prior to the intervention, and would help us know if posttest differences were the result of something other than the experimental procedure.

Next we will look at two designs with a single group. The first uses a pretest–posttest design and is quasi-experimental, because it has multiple waves of measurement. In the first one-group design, after the pretest (O_1), the group gets the intervention (X), followed by the posttest (O_2). We could evaluate our anxiety treatment by giving a pretest, administering the treatment, and giving a posttest —without comparisons to a control group.

Pretest-Posttest Non-experiment

O_1	X	O_2

By comparison to the next design we will look at, this design has the advantage of a pretest for our group, helping us evaluate how much change occurs as a result of the intervention. What we don't know is how much of the change could be related to the measurement process itself, as we can do when we have a control group.

The second one-group design is a simple posttest-only design. There is only an intervention and a posttest, which makes it a non-experimental design. Sometimes this is called a pre-experimental design.

Posttest Only Non-Experiment

X	O

You might use this last design if you want to study the effects of a natural disaster like a flood or tornado, and you want to do so by interviewing survivors. In this design, you don't have a comparison group, for example, doing interviews in a nearby town that didn't have the tornado. You also don't have multiple waves of measurement, for example, a pre-tornado level of how people in the damaged town were doing.

Are non-experimental studies worthwhile? Of course! You can gain valuable information by well-conducted post-disaster surveys. But you may have a hard time establishing which of the things you observed are due to the disaster rather than to other factors, like the peculiarities of the town or pre-disaster characteristics. This kind of study would help in narrowing down the factors to study more rigorously in a controlled experiment.

We do not want to belittle a study that is not a true experiment. True experiments are not always possible under the circumstances or at our present level of knowledge. We just need to be cautious in how we interpret studies with less rigorous designs, for example, looking for other confirmations of the findings or not generalizing much beyond the sample. And we need to remember that if we are looking for cause and effect, we need a research design that can show that information.

Is there a control group? If so, how was it obtained?

A **control group** in a study is a group comparable to the **experimental group** that does not receive the experimental treatment. Not all research designs require a control group, and a control is not always possible. However, some experts would say a research design is not a true experiment unless it includes a comparison or control group, as well as random assignment. It is true that a control group increases our confidence in the internal validity of a study; it helps assure that changes in the experimental group are the result of the experimental manipulation and not a function of the way the dependent variable was measured.

Sometimes finding another group that is strictly comparable is not possible. In some medical research, for example, withholding certain basic treatment is not considered ethical. In cases such as this, a *comparison group* may be used instead, a group not strictly a control but at least somewhat comparable. For instance, if you are studying a new medical procedure, you could sample people receiving the usual or routine treatment as a comparison group. This avoids unethically providing no treatment at all to a control group in a study of a new treatment.

When an experimenter establishes a control group, the hope is that the experimental group and the control group will be equivalent on all variables except the independent variable. Control groups can be established in a variety of ways.

- The easiest and surest way of scrambling all possible variables across groups is random assignment of participants to the experimental and control groups.

- In a matched group design, participants are formed into pairs of so-called "twins" that are matched on key variables. To do this well requires extremely large samples, so that pairs really are alike on many variables. Researchers sometimes cut corners and only match on a few variables, so as you read a study using this procedure, you need to be convinced that the groups are well matched, and that other variables that are not controlled for are not confounding the study.

- In an equated-groups design, group equivalence is established by comparing means, medians, or percentages of the groups on important participant variables. This is a much simpler procedure than matching

---

Learning Key

Control group: Group in a study comparable to an experimental group but that does not receive the experimental treatment.

Experimental group: Group in a study that does receive an experimental treatment.

153

participants, but you will need to determine if what was done is likely to have yielded equivalent groups. Typically the researcher will compare the means, medians, or percentages of the two groups and tell us they are not significantly different. Ideally, the two groups should be not only not significantly different, but they also should be significantly the same (p > .95). The important thing is to look at the differences between the groups before treatment begins to see if any differences between them seem to be meaningful. If there are differences between groups that are discovered before treatment begins, dropping, adding, or exchanging participants can sometimes bring the groups into better balance.

- Another way to avoid nonequivalence of groups is to keep the sample narrow by restricting it to a homogenous group of participants, such as limiting the sample to female, Caucasian, college graduates aged 25 to 35 with high IQs. The price one pays for reducing possible confounding variables this way is limiting the generalizability of the study.

- Another control group procedure is to have participants serve as their own control, that is, have the same people serve as both the experimental and control group. This only works in some situations, and even then may be problematic because exposure to the first experience may change the participants in a way that affects their response to the second experience. When this kind of procedure is used, it is important that the researcher randomly counterbalances the treatment conditions so that some people get Treatment A first and others get Treatment B first.

- Sometimes researchers who discover factors that make groups nonequivalent will use statistical techniques to compensate, such as using the analysis of covariance, a variation on analysis of variance that takes correlations into account. Sometimes the variable on which there are differences can be treated as an additional experimental variable.

Whatever technique is used to create a control or comparison group, you need to evaluate whether the author's explanation makes sense and whether it is reasonable to expect that the groups are equivalent in important respects other than the independent variable.

Is the design suitable to test the hypotheses and does it answer the research question?

Now that you have looked at both the type of research question that is asked and the nature of the research design, you are in a position to consider whether there is a match between the two. Most critical is whether the research question is one of

154

causality, and if so, whether the research design yields a true experiment, because the search for a cause cannot be fully addressed with less than a true experiment.

But beyond the matter of the match between question and design is the fit between research question, hypotheses, and research design. Does the design follow from the question and does it accurately address the hypotheses? For example, if the question is causal, is the design a true experiment? If the question is relational, is the design at least a quasi-experiment, and do the hypotheses answer a relational question? Common sense is as important here as technical research know-how as you look at the match between question, hypotheses, and design.

Are the methods and procedures clearly described in sufficient detail to be understood and replicated?

How complete is the description of what the researcher did? Do you understand reasonably well what was done? Would another researcher be able to do a similar study based on what is described? We don't need every minute detail, but we need to know the general outlines of what was done.

Now that we have seen how the researcher plans to answer the research question, we are ready to see what results are reported in the results section, how they are interpreted in the discussion section, and how the study is summarized in the abstract. We look first at the results.

9

Reading the Results, Discussion, and Abstract

Reading the Results Section

In part I of this book you learned about descriptive and inferential statistics. As you read the results section of a research article, you have the opportunity to use your knowledge of statistics.

While many readers simply skip over the results section, you will not want to be one of them. It simply is not wise to assume that all the conclusions discussed later about this section will be accurately drawn. We will want to consider these questions as we look at the results of a study:

- Do descriptive statistics and tests of significance appear to have been used appropriately? Are there any obvious errors in calculation or presentation of the results?

- Are tables and figures clearly labeled and accurately presented?

Overview

The **results section** objectively describes what the study found by presenting the data and the statistical analyses. Usually the descriptive statistics are presented first, followed by the inferential statistics. Tables and figures are often used to convey important information in an organized manner.

In the **results section** we expect to find a full and objective presentation of the findings in the study, with all the results, whether they confirm the hypotheses or not. Included will be both descriptive statistics (means, standard deviations, correlations, and so forth) and inferential statistics (such as t-tests, ANOVAs, or Chi-Squares, each with their degrees of freedom and the level of significance achieved or not achieved).

Do descriptive statistics and tests of significance appear to have been used appropriately? Are there any obvious errors in calculation or presentation of the results?

The more you know about statistics, the easier it will be to spot problems in the results, but do not be intimidated if you are feeling rusty or you are new to analyzing statistical information. There are a variety of things you can be looking for. Do you see any obvious errors in calculation or presentation, like percentages that don't add up to 100, or group Ns that don't add up to the total N? Are the statistical techniques that are used consistent with the level of measurement the measures provide? For example, t-tests and ANOVA require interval data. Did the researcher measure on a continuous scale, but then collapse the data into very limited categories for analysis, such as measuring IQs on an interval scale, but collapsing data into *above 100* and *below 100*? There may be theoretical rationales available for the way data are handled, but be curious about the possibility that the usual way of handling the data did not provide significance, while an unusual way did provide significance.

When a study does pre- and post-treatment testing on participants, the data comparing the groups is often in the form of change scores—the difference between each individual's pretest and posttest scores. If the groups differ in pre-treatment score levels, those differences may impact the change scores in unanticipated ways. Suppose a 320-pound person loses 20 pounds, and a 120-pound person loses 20 pounds. Their change scores would be the same, 20 pounds.

Learning Key

Results section: Objective description and statistical analysis of data found in the study.

Discussion section: Review, interpretation, and evaluation of study results.

Abstract: Brief summary of a research journal article, located at the beginning of the article.

However, it is obvious that those 20 pounds mean something quite different for these two people. Does the author adequately account for problems such as this when change scores are used? Recall the problem with the reliability of change scores we saw in chapter 4: When we are measuring the change between scores on two different tests or two different administrations of the same test, there is unreliability in each administration which is compounded in the calculation of the change score. When two different tests are used, the reliability of the results can be even further reduced by the correlation between the two tests. Thus, if change scores are used, we need to ask if unreliability of the change scores might be a factor in how the results came out.

Another issue can arise if a researcher uses lack of significance to indicate that two pre-treatment groups in an experiment are equivalent. For example, if the researcher finds lack of significance in differences in scores of men and of women on a particular test, it doesn't mean men and women are the same on this characteristic. It only means that in this instance there was not a statistically significant difference. Watch for any overreaching conclusions in statements about significance.

Readers need to be particularly alert for Type I errors. If many significance tests are performed, the odds increase that some of the results will be statistically significant by chance alone. Remember that if we are using a .05 significance level, 5 of every 100 significance tests performed may be significant by chance alone. I once reviewed an article someone had submitted for publication in which 60 correlation coefficients were calculated, of which only 2 were significantly greater than zero. We would have expected 3 to be significant by chance alone at the .05 level of significance ($60 \times .05 = 3$). Needless to say, I did not recommend publication of that article, because it seems likely the significant results were due to chance.

To avoid this problem, there are special techniques that compensate for the use of many tests of significance, which a researcher will describe if used. It is also important that the researcher decide ahead of time which comparisons are most important, and then limit the number of significance tests performed. In the study mentioned in the previous paragraph, some of the 60 correlations were not crucial to the study. Looking only at the ones that were central to the research question would have reduced the Type I error risk.

Remember that *significant* does not mean important. As you review the results and the later discussion sections, look for the size of the effects of the independent variable in terms of meaningfulness. If a sample is large enough, very small differences can be statistically significant, while very small samples may have difficulty achieving significance even when the effects seem substantial. For example, with a large sample the difference between two groups might be statistically significant when the difference in the means of the two groups was only 2 points on a 250 point scale. We can wonder how meaningful that finding is. The expectation is that researchers will tell us not only that results were significant, but also give us information about how meaningful these findings are. Look for discussion of *effect size* in the results or discussion sections.

Are tables and figures clearly labeled and accurately presented?

Tables and figures should make the results easier to grasp, but whether or not they do that is our concern here. Titles, headings, labels, and captions should be clear and understandable. The contents of figures or graphs need to make the results clear, without distorting them or misleading the reader.

In some graphs there is distortion of scale, which makes differences between groups appear to be larger than they really are, by magnifying a small portion of the scale or makes differences appear smaller than they really are. Figure 9.1 illustrates how even being technically accurate is sometimes not helpful. Imagine we are reading a medical study in which two groups differ in their mean body temperature. Group A has a mean body temperature of 98.6 degrees while Group B has a mean temperature of 101.4 degrees. If we were measuring temperatures in some non-medical situations, a difference in temperature between 98.6 degrees and 101.4 degrees would not seem like much difference, and that is what we notice in the graph on the left in figure 9.1, which displays temperature from 0 to 100 degrees. It appears that the two groups are not very different. However, in medicine a body temperature of 98.6 is the normal value, and 101.4 is distinctly elevated. For a medical study, the graph on the right, which plots the percentage of people in each group whose temperature exceeds the normal 98.6, presents a more meaningful view of the information and makes clear that there is a practically significant as well as a statistically significant difference between the groups.

If figures, graphs, and tables are used in the article, look for displays that aid understanding in a meaningful and accurate way, without distortion.

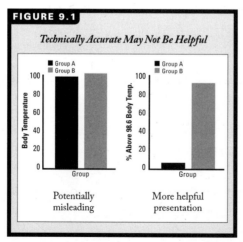

FIGURE 9.1

Technically Accurate May Not Be Helpful

Potentially misleading

More helpful presentation

Diagrams from *Critical Thinking About Research* by J. Meltzoff, published by American Psychological Association, Washington, D.C., 1998. Reprinted with permission.

Reading the Discussion Section

The discussion section of a study begins with a narrow focus on the findings of the study and then proceeds more broadly with conclusions and future implications. This is the only section of the research article where it is appropriate for the author's opinions to show through. The expectation is that the writing throughout the rest of the article will be strictly objective. We will want to consider these questions as we read the discussion section:

- Are the original research questions addressed in the discussion section? Are new questions addressed that did not appear in the introduction? Does the author address whether or not each of the hypotheses was supported or refuted?

- Does the author make appropriate generalizations to different groups of people and/or situations? Is the author's interpretation of the findings consistent with the type of research design used in the study?

- Does the author do an adequate job of pointing out the limitations of the study?

Overview

The **discussion section** reviews, interprets, and evaluates the results of the study. The review of the results is desirably done in nontechnical language, using no statistical markings or jargon. Discussion sections typically

- list the hypotheses and state if the results supported or contradicted them,

- discuss similarities and differences between the current findings and findings of previous research,

- cite weaknesses of the current study and make suggestions for improving the research design, and

- provide suggestions for future research.

In the **discussion section**, we will be looking for a jargon-free review, interpretation, and evaluation of the findings. The researcher draws inferences from the data, generalizes from them, and states conclusions. Here the hypotheses are accepted or rejected, the findings are considered in relation to any theory being tested and previous studies cited in the literature review, and differences found are explained. It is not only permissible but appropriate for the author's own views to be expressed here.

However, we will expect modest, evenhanded, and candid discussion, not over-reaching, biased misinterpretation of the data or disregard of unfavorable results.

Are the original research questions addressed in the discussion section? Are any new questions addressed that did not appear in the Introduction? Does the author address whether or not each of the hypotheses were supported or refuted?

We will expect the original research question and the hypotheses to be addressed specifically in the discussion, although they may also have been addressed in the results section. You will want to look for yourself to see whether the hypotheses and the data match up, and whether the researcher's interpretation of the results makes sense, given the information you have gathered to this point.

This is particularly the case when results do not coincide well with predictions. It is understandable that researchers may be reluctant to give up on cherished beliefs. When the data don't support the author's ideas, explanations and justifications may become strained. Even when predicted results are obtained, conclusions and generalizations sometimes go beyond the data.

Sometimes totally new research questions appear in the discussion, presumably because the findings were not as expected and the researcher wants to find an explanation. While it is appropriate to learn from our research and get ideas for new research, new research questions occurring at this point in an article tend to suggest something amiss. The proper way to handle findings that are not what the researcher expected is to report what was found, offer any possible explanations thought to be pertinent, and make suggestions for later research, not make up a new question for this study.

All of the hypotheses should be addressed in the discussion, even those that were not supported. Sometimes articles talk only about what was supported, as though unsupported hypotheses didn't matter. In well-designed research, we can learn from what does not work as well as what does.

Does the author make appropriate generalizations to different groups of people and/or situations? Is the author's interpretation of the findings consistent with the type of research design used in the study?

It is appropriate for the researcher to draw implications from the results, suggesting what they may mean and ways they can be generalized. Your task is to see if the inferences and generalizations are supported by the data.

Even when predicted results are obtained, conclusions and generalizations may go far beyond the data. Meltzoff (1998) offers two examples. Suppose a researcher states that men are better at abstract reasoning than women, after a study comparing thirty male college seniors with thirty female college seniors, all of whom were psychology majors at the university where the researcher teaches. While the means on the test of abstract reasoning used were significantly different at the .05 level, generalizing from this sample to all men and women is not warranted. It is sufficient to say that in a sample of college senior psychology majors, men scored higher on a particular abstract reasoning test. Before this finding is ready for general application, other studies will need to be done to show similar results with other kinds of samples and with other measures of abstract reasoning.

Or suppose another researcher compares the productivity of thirty workers assembling small electronic components in the morning and afternoon. Finding productivity for these workers significantly higher in the morning than in the afternoon on twenty-five consecutive workdays, he concludes, "People are more productive in the morning than they are in the afternoon." Generalization to *people* is not warranted based on this small sample, and the type of work being done here cannot be generalized to all other factory work, much less unrelated types of activity. It is sufficient to describe these results modestly and let the results of other studies help define the general applicability.

Of particular concern is a researcher's claim that causality has been demonstrated. Causality can only be suggested when one has a *true experimental design*, often with a control group, and usually with a reasonably representative and unbiased sample.

Does the author do an adequate job of pointing out the limitations of the study?

The researcher should discuss study limitations and how these limitations may have affected the results. Included would be such things as limitations in the research design, complications in the sampling procedures, weaknesses in the measurement instruments, and other factors that may have compromised the internal or external validity of the study. This is not a time for true confessions, in which the researcher apologizes for every possible weakness in the study, but rather a place where major limitations are identified and discussed, so readers can make up their own minds about the value of the study.

Limitations to note might include a small or not very representative sample (only psychology majors in one small urban university, for example), attrition, failure to have validity checks for the manipulation, and so forth. Particularly pertinent here are unforeseen complications that arose during the course of the study and that may have impacted the results. Potentially important variables that were not controlled in the study design (perhaps that only became clear during the course of the study) should also be noted. For example, in the study cited earlier about support for military families (page 146), the deployment of the soldiers from one base would certainly need to be noted.

Evaluating the Abstract

The abstract is at the beginning of an article, but still it is a summary, and *conceptually* comes at the end of the article. This is why we cannot evaluate the abstract until we understand the whole article. Our final question in reading a research article is this:

Does the abstract adequately convey the essence of the study?

Overview

The **abstract** is a concise summary of the research question and hypotheses, the sample, the methodology, statistical analyses, results, and implications of the study. It is important that this is done well, since it provides an overview for the reader and often is the only part of the study that some readers will see.

At the beginning of chapter 7, we noted that although an **abstract** is at the beginning of a research article, conceptually it is the final summary of the article. Therefore, we now consider the abstract. A well-written abstract is important because people doing online searches on a topic often use only the article's title and abstract to decide whether or not the article is relevant.

The abstract is a brief summary (up to 120 words is the typical length) of the entire article, providing the reader with a quick overview of the article's content. A good abstract contains a concise summary of (a) the article's problem or research question and hypotheses, (b) information about the participants, (c) a brief review of the method used, (d) the statistical analyses and results of the study, and (e) the implications of the study. Unfortunately, not all abstracts have all this information.

Does the abstract adequately convey the essence of the study?

Now that you have thoroughly reviewed the article, you will be able to judge how well the author has performed the important task of summarizing all the sections of the article. As you read research articles, you may be amazed at how many authors fail to do the job well. Of particular concern are those who claim too much or do not acknowledge crucial limitations.

Because the abstract is at the beginning of an article, some authors are tempted to include introductory material. However, because the abstract is actually a summary, it is never appropriate for an abstract to tell what a study is *going to do*. It is not an introduction in any way.

The more experience you have reading articles, the more you will be convinced of the wisdom of this simple rule: *Never use only the abstract when reporting information on a topic—read the whole article*. Use the abstract as a *starting point* to help you with the rest of the article.

You're On Your Way

In these pages we have seen how statistics can describe or summarize data that has been collected. We have seen how inferential statistics help us know whether that data can be generalized by telling us how likely the differences in those data could have happened by chance alone. We have seen how information about the reliability and validity of instruments we are interested in can help us know whether the instruments are consistent in what they measure and whether they measure what they are intended to measure. We have seen that the correlation coefficients reporting this reliability and validity information look like percentages, but that those numbers must be squared to convert them into familiar percentage form. We have considered the fairly predictable structure of research articles and how statistics and measurement knowledge can be applied to understanding professional research.

Armed with this greater understanding of statistics and measurement, and with an overview of what to look for in research articles, you are ready to confidently expand your use of professional literature and assessment instruments. Best wishes as you strive to develop your interests and professional skills and stay up-to-date.

APPENDIX

A Brief Introduction to Personality Type

Many examples in this book involve personality type as measured by the Myers-Briggs Type Indicator® (MBTI®) instrument. The MBTI instrument was developed by Isabel Briggs Myers based on the psychological type theories of Carl G. Jung as modified by her mother, Katharine C. Briggs. This brief introduction to personality type may help you better understand some of the examples in this book.

The MBTI instrument helps a person identify a preference between two opposite alternatives on each of four aspects of personality. The theory underlying the instrument is that we have consistent, enduring mental patterns in how we prefer to direct the focus of our attention and energy, in what kind of information we seek, in what we use as our primary basis to make decisions, and in how we prefer to structure our lives and orient ourselves to the world around us. The theory is based on the premise that our preferences in mental patterns are like our preference for using one hand over the other. When we use a preference, the experience tends to seem comfortable and natural. We can and do use our nonpreferences, but that often seems awkward, slow, or something that requires extra effort and concentration, although sometimes we have learned to use a nonpreference so well or are so fascinated by a nonpreference that we do not readily recognize which is our natural preference and which is a learned skill.

The first alternatives of personality type, Extraversion and Introversion, relate to one's orientation to the world and how one is energized. Extraverts tend to be energized by the stimuli of people, activities, and things in the world around them, while Introverts tend to draw energy from their inner life of reflections, memories, and ideas.

Sensing and Intuition are called perception functions and identify the kind of information we tend to seek first and trust most. People who prefer Sensing tend to seek facts; specifics; what is real, concrete, and practical. People who prefer Intuition tend to seek underlying meanings, associations between facts, possibilities, and patterns.

Thinking and Feeling are called judgment functions and describe the primary basis for evaluating information as we make decisions. People who prefer Thinking tend to base decisions on logic, analysis, a set of criteria, and cause-and-effect reasoning. People who prefer Feeling tend to base decisions on the impact on people, on person-centered values, on personal and humane concerns.

The alternatives of Judging and Perceiving relate to our preferred lifestyle and to our orientation to the outer world. People who prefer Judging tend to prefer a lifestyle that is scheduled, planned, and organized. The public face of a person who prefers Judging is one of being decisive. For the person who prefers Judging, the part of the personality that others are likely to see first is the person's preferred judgment function of Thinking or Feeling. People who prefer Perceiving tend to prefer a lifestyle that is flexible, adaptable, and spontaneous. The public face of a person who prefers Perceiving is one of being open to new information. For the person who prefers Perceiving, the part of the personality that others are likely to see first is the person's preferred perception function of Sensing or Intuition.

Identifying one preference among each of the four sets of alternatives results in a four-letter type code. All the possible combinations of preferences result in sixteen different but equally valuable types.

Type, however, is more than simply adding together the preferences. Each part of the type interacts in a dynamic way with each other part to make the whole type.

The heart or core of the personality type are the two kinds of perception functions used for gathering information—Sensing and Intuition—and the two kinds of judgment functions used for making decisions—Thinking and Feeling. We can and do use all four of these functions, although we prefer two of them and these two are the middle letters of our type code. For each type the Sensing, Intuition, Thinking, and Feeling have a specific order of preferred use.

The number one function is called the dominant function and is the motivating, governing, unifying force of the personality. It is used in our preferred world. Extraverts extravert the dominant function. Introverts introvert the dominant function. Typically this dominant function develops in childhood. The number two function complements the dominant function and typically develops in adolescence. Between the first two functions, one gives us a preferred way to gather information and the other a preferred way to make decisions. One gives us a way to interact with the world around us in an extraverted way. It is what others are likely to see and hear first in us. The other gives us a way to interact with our inner world in an introverted way. It is what we tend to think through inside our heads.

The number three and four functions do not appear in our type code. Typically they develop in adulthood as we have need for them and opportunity to learn skill in using them.

When you understand the dynamic nature of type, you recognize that a type code gives you several pieces of information about a person. If I tell you that my type code is ISFJ, you know that I have preferences for Introversion, Sensing, Feeling, and Judging. Because my type ends with J you know that my public face is one of being decisive, and that when people first meet me, they often recognize my concern for people and for harmony among people. You know that because the Feeling function that you see publicly is extraverted, my Sensing function is introverted. You know that because I have a preference for Introversion, my dominant function is introverted. You know that the motivating and most important part of my personality is the satisfaction I have in keeping track of and organizing facts and the details of life. You may recognize that the interaction between my dominant introverted Sensing and my complementary extraverted Feeling function influences my passion for wanting to make concepts of statistics and measurement understandable to people!

This brief introduction may give you some context for the examples of statistical and measurement concepts based on the MBTI instrument.

APPENDIX 3

More Significance Tests Illustrated

In chapter 3 we illustrated the way significance tests work by demonstrating the use of the **t-test** when we are comparing two *means*. In this appendix we illustrate several other widely used significance tests. The t-test is appropriate not only when we want to compare the means of two groups, but also when we want to determine whether a *correlation coefficient* is significantly different from zero. We will check the correlation coefficient we calculated in chapter 2 to see if it is significant.

When we have more than two groups in a study, we can't use the t test, but the **analysis of variance (ANOVA)** serves our purpose. We will illustrate both a one-way and a two-way ANOVA as we explore applications of the XYZ test we met in chapter 3.

Sometimes our data are only frequencies or counts (nominal data), in which case **chi-square** is the appropriate significance test. We will explore preferences for ice cream flavors as we see how chi-square works.

t-test for Correlation Coefficients

Whenever we correlate any two variables, we are likely to get at least a small positive or negative correlation in that particular sample, just by chance. We use the t-test to help us know if a correlation coefficient we obtain is bigger than chance alone could explain.

Hypotheses. To illustrate the use of a t-test for a correlation, let's check to see if our correlation between height and weight in 10 eight-year-olds was significantly greater than zero. Looking back at table 2.5 on page 33, we see the r (correlation coefficient) was .76. Our null hypothesis is that the population correlation is zero. Our research hypothesis is that the correlation is enough greater than zero that it is not just a chance finding.

Test of Significance and Level of Significance. In testing the significance of our correlation of heights and weights, we will use the t-test. We can use a one-tailed test because there obviously is not a negative relationship between height and weight, and we set our minimum alpha level at .05.

Degrees of freedom. Calculation of a correlation takes away 2 degrees of freedom instead of the 1 degree of freedom (d.f.) we took away in calculating the mean, because we are estimating 2 parameters in a correlation—the standard deviations of the two variables, SD_X and SD_Y. There is greater limitation on our data because a correlation represents the relationship between *two* variables, not just a calculation about *one* variable.

Determining t. To find the t for a test of significance of a correlation coefficient (r), this formula is used:

$$t = \frac{r\sqrt{N-2}}{\sqrt{1-r^2}}$$

We multiply our correlation by the square root of the degrees of freedom and divide by the square root of 1 minus the correlation coefficient squared.

For our height and weight correlation,

$$t = \frac{.76\sqrt{10-2}}{\sqrt{1-.76^2}} = \frac{.76\sqrt{8}}{\sqrt{1-.58}} = \frac{2.14}{.65} = 3.29$$

For 8 (N - 2) d.f. and alpha = .05 (one-tailed), the critical value of t is 1.860. We can legitimately use a one-tailed test here because we are asking if the correlation is significantly greater than zero; the direction of the correlation is not a concern at this point. Any t value over 1.860 will tell us our correlation is significant. Since we found a t of 3.29, our correlation of .76 is significantly greater than zero. Indeed, we can see in a t table that any t greater that 2.896 is significant at the .01 level with a one-tailed test, so we can put two asterisks after our finding: t = 3.29**

Let's summarize the steps we took in applying the t-test to our height-and-weight correlation.

- We stated our hypotheses.
- We chose the statistical test to use, the t-test.
- We determined we would use a one-tailed test, with a minimum level of significance of .05.

- We determined our degrees of freedom to be N - 2.
- We applied the formula for t, multiplying our correlation by the square root of the d.f., and divided by the square root of 1 minus the correlation squared (the variance accounted for).
- We looked in a table of t to find the critical value for our degrees of freedom.
- Because the result we found (3.29) was greater than the critical value of t at the .01 level, we reported that our correlation is significant at the .01 level.

Analysis of Variance

Let's return now to consideration of the XYZ Inventory, introduced in chapter 3. After our great success with comparing Es and Is, let's suppose we decide to test some proposition related to the relative performance on the XYZ Inventory of people with the four different dominant functions, Sensing (S), Intuition (N), Thinking (T), and Feeling (F). While the t-test served us well in our earlier experiment comparing two groups, it will not work acceptably in comparing *more than* two groups. For this situation we need the Analysis of Variance (ANOVA), one of the most widely used statistical techniques in behavioral research. ANOVA, also called the F-test, is used to test the differences among *three or more* means.

Hypotheses. In our new experiment, the null hypothesis is that the differences between the means of the groups are small enough that the groups could have come from the same, single population, not different populations related to dominant function. Our research hypothesis is that the differences between groups are real. If our results are significant and we reject the null hypothesis, we can assume these groups were not samples from the same population but that they are samples from different populations—in other words, that there really are differences in XYZ scores between people with different dominant functions.

Getting a significant F doesn't tell us which differences in means are significant, only that significant differences exist. When necessary, special significance tests can be used to determine *which* differences are significant, but that gets beyond the scope of this introduction.

Level of significance. As with our t-test, before we begin our experiment we must not only state our hypotheses, but we must also state our minimally-acceptable level of significance. Again we will set our level of significance or alpha at .05. We do not need to make a decision about a one-tailed or two-tailed test in ANOVA. We use one-tailed tests in ANOVA because we are asking only if there are more differences than chance could account for, and are not asking which differences are greater.

Collecting data. We give the XYZ Inventory to groups of 10 sophomores known to be dominant on each of the four functions (Sensing, Intuition, Thinking, Feeling) and get the following means for the four groups:

Group	Group Mean
Ss	47.54
Ns	66.06
Ts	53.14
Fs	57.98
Grand Mean	56.18 *(Grand Mean is mean for all participants, in all groups)*

We can see that there are some differences between the four sample means. We also know that whenever we take samples from a population, there will be some differences due to sampling error. Are the differences between our four groups so small that the four groups could just be samples from the same population of scores (in which dominant function has no effect on XYZ scores), or are the differences in means great enough that we can conclude there really are differences between dominant functions on the XYZ Inventory? ANOVA helps us answer this question by measuring the differences in the means relative to the amount of underlying variability within each group. To keep our example simple, we are using groups of the same size. If we did not have equal size groups, calculations for ANOVA would have to be adjusted; statistics books provide various formulas we can use depending on the nature of our data.

Variance. As we introduce the Analysis of Variance, let's review our definition of variance. In chapter 2 we described variance as a measure of variability, the spread of scores around the central point of a distribution. The variance is the standard deviation squared, SD^2. Because it is not in the same unit of measurement as our data, the variance is generally not a helpful descriptive statistic. However, it measures everything that is happening in our data—all experimental effects and all sources of error—and can be partitioned or divided into each of its component parts. When we considered variance accounted for (r^2) on p. 34–36, we saw that variance could be partitioned into two component parts, the part attributable to the correlation between variables and the part that is related to other factors. In ANOVA and other advanced techniques, variance is used because it measures *all* the differences we are studying, or experimental effects, as well as all the sources of error including chance factors unrelated to our experiment, and we are able to divide the variance into component parts.

Within-groups and between-groups variance. In an analysis of variance, we will find two independent estimates of the variance of the scores in the study:

- an estimate of variability within groups (in our example, within the groups of Ss, Ns, Ts, and Fs) called within-groups variance, and

- an estimate of the variability between the groups (in our experiment, due to the differences between the Ss, Ns, Ts, and Fs) called the between-groups variance.

Because all the people within the same group have the same experimental characteristic or get the same treatment—in this experiment, they have the same dominant function—we can consider all the within-groups variance to be error variance. This *error variance* would include

- sampling error (our participants do not perfectly represent people with each dominant function),

- the unreliability of the test (the XYZ is not perfect), and

- the influence of variables other than dominant function that effect scores (some people get high or low XYZ scores for other reasons).

Between-groups variance includes all of the same components of error variance as the within-groups variance but, in addition, the between-groups variance includes the effects of the independent variable, that is, actual differences between the four groups.

$$F = \frac{SD^2_B}{SD^2_W} \quad (SD^2 = \text{variance})$$

We will use the ratio between these two variance estimates to test the significance of our results, dividing the variance between groups by the variance within groups. In effect the formula allows us to cancel out the error variance, leaving the amount of effect of the independent variable, that is, any actual differences between the groups. This is illustrated on page 176.

In analysis of variance, our reference for judging the size of our ratio of between-groups and within-groups variability is provided by the F distribution. The F statistic is actually a close cousin of the t statistic. We can say that $F = t^2$ if we had only two groups, and t with an infinite number of d.f. is equal to the z statistic and the normal distribution.

Sum of Squares. A basic concept in the analysis of variance is the sum of squares. In figuring the variance (SD^2), we take the deviation of each score from the mean and square it. When we add up these squared deviations we have the sum of squares.

$$F = \frac{SD^2_B}{SD^2_W}$$

We will use sums of squares to find the two kinds of variance needed in our F-test formula. Because our formula includes variance within groups and variance between groups, we need to calculate within-groups sum of squares (SS_W) and between-groups sum of squares (SS_B).

To illustrate calculation of sums of squares, let's over-simplify some scores for our four groups and consider groups with only four participants each. The following are *raw scores* on the abbreviated XYZ Inventory:

F-ratio Cancels Out Error

To illustrate the way in which our F ratio *cancels out* the error, let's look at our formula a different way.

$$F = \frac{\text{Variance Between}}{\text{Variance Within}} = \frac{\text{error + actual differences}}{\text{error}} = \text{differences}$$

Because F is a ratio, the closer to 1.00 that the F-ratio is, the less effect the difference between groups has. For example, if there is no effect on our XYZ scores from differences in dominant function, so that we are measuring only error (to which we will arbitrarily assign a value of 2), our formula might look like this:

$$F = \frac{2+0}{2} = \frac{2}{2} = 1$$

If there are differences between groups that effect XYZ scores, our formula instead might look like this:

$$F = \frac{2+8}{2} = \frac{10}{2} = 5$$

This actually is very similar to what we did in the t-test to determine the significance between two means. We divided the difference between the first mean and the second mean (which is a measure of the *variability* between the two groups) by the standard error of the difference (a measure of the variability *within* the two groups because it is based on the standard error of both groups).

$$t = \frac{\text{Mean}_1 - \text{Mean}_2}{S_{diff}}$$

	S	N	T	F
	3	7	4	5
	2	5	3	4
	2	4	3	4
	1	4	2	3
ΣX	8	20	12	16
$\overline{X}$	2	5	3	4

$$\text{Grand Mean} = \frac{8+20+12+16}{16} = \frac{56}{16} = 3.5$$

To find the SS_W we take each person's score and subtract it from the mean of its group. Because we are only interested in the amount of the deviation, and because we will square our deviations in the next step, we can skip the minus signs. We get the following *deviations from individual group means:*

1	2	1	1
0	0	0	0
0	1	0	0
1	1	1	1

Squaring these deviations we get the following squared deviations from individual group means:

1	4	1	1	
0	0	0	0	
0	1	0	0	
1	1	1	1	
2	**6**	**2**	**2**	$SS_W = 2 + 6 + 2 + 2 = 12$

Adding the sums at the bottom of the four columns we get our sum of squares within groups (SS_W), which is 12.

Next we find the sum of squares between the groups. The between-groups sum of squares (SS_B) is found by subtracting the grand mean from each group mean, squaring the result, multiplying by the N (number of individuals) in the group, and adding the terms for all groups together.

$$SS_B = (\overline{X} - GM)^2 (N) + \dots \text{ for each group.}$$
$$= (2\text{-}3.5)^2 (4) + (5\text{-}3.5)^2 (4) + (3\text{-}3.5)^2 (4) + (4\text{-}3.5)^2 (4)$$
$$= 2.25 (4) + 2.25 (4) + .25 (4) + .25 (4)$$
$$= 9 + 9 + 1 + 1 = 20$$

Degrees of freedom. Before we can find the variance estimates, we need to know how many degrees of freedom we have for each sum of squares. Because we have 16 participants in these calculations, 4 in each of 4 groups, our N is 16. The total degrees of freedom available is N - 1 or 15. One d.f. is lost from the total due to the estimate of the grand mean.

The between-groups degrees of freedom is the number of groups (K) minus 1. There are four groups in our experiment so K = 4, and we have 4 - 1 or 3 d.f. between groups. Again, 1 d.f. is lost due to the grand mean.

The degrees of freedom within groups is the total N for all groups combined, minus K. One d.f. is lost for each sample mean. For our experiment, we had a total N of 16 and a K of 4, so SS_W has 16 - 4, or 12 d.f. *Our SS_W also happened to be 12, so when we see the number 12 in our examples below for this particular hypothetical experiment, we will need to pay attention to whether the number refers to SS_W or to $d.f._W$.*

Finding the variance estimates. Once we have our sums of squares and know the degrees of freedom, we can find the variance estimates, also called *mean squares*, of the sum of squares within groups (SS_W), and the sum of squares between groups (SS_B).

The *variance between groups* is the sum of squares between (20) divided by the between-groups d.f. (3), or 6.67.

$$\text{variance between groups} = \frac{\text{sum of squares between}}{\text{degrees of freedom}}$$

$$SD^2_B = \frac{SS_B}{K-1} = \frac{20}{3} = 6.67$$

The variance within groups is the sum of squares within (12), divided by the within-groups d.f. (12), or 1.00.

$$SD^2_W = \frac{SS_W}{N-K} = \frac{12}{12} = 1$$

Finding the F-ratio. Now we are ready to find the F-ratio we need to test the significance of our results. It is found by dividing the variance between by the variance within.

$$F = \frac{SD^2_B}{SD^2_W} = \frac{6.67}{1.00} = 6.67$$

The following table summarizes the steps we took to achieve our F-ratio:

Source of variation	Sum of Squares	d.f.	Variance estimate	F
Between groups	20	3 (K-1)	6.67	6.67
Within groups	12	12 (N-K)	1.00	

To determine the significance of our results, we look up the critical value of F in a Table of F in a statistics book. We use the d.f. of *both* the between- and within- groups variances to find the right critical value. For 3 and 12 degrees of freedom, we find that the critical value of F is 3.49 at the .05 level of significance and 5.95 at the .01 level. Because our F of 6.67 is larger than the critical value, we can reject the null hypothesis, which was that the means we found are from random samples from the same population. We can conclude that there *are* differences in XYZ scores based on differences in dominant function.

We can state that our results are significant at the .01 level. We specified that we would not accept any result that was not significant at least at the .05 level, but because the F we got exceeded the critical value for p < .01, we can claim that.

These are the steps we took in using the F test or ANOVA in our experiment with dominant function groups and scores on the XYZ Inventory.

- We stated our hypotheses.

- We chose the statistical test to use, the F test.

- We set our minimal level of significance at .05.

- We determined our degrees of freedom to be K-1 for the variance between and N-K for the variance within.

- We found the estimate of between-groups variance by finding the SS_B and dividing it by the d.f._B.

- We found the estimate of within-groups variance by finding the SS_W and dividing it by the d.f._W.

- We found the F ratio by dividing the between-groups variance by the within-groups variance.

- We looked at a table of F to find the critical value for our degrees of freedom.

- Because the result we found (6.67) was greater than the critical value of F at the .05 level (3.26) and also greater than the critical value of F at the .01 level (5.41), we reported that there were differences in XYZ scores based on differences in dominant function, significant at the .01 level.

With-Groups SS and Between-Groups SS Equal the Total SS

We have said that variance is divisible into component parts. We have calculated sums of squares within groups and between groups. These two sums of squares add up to the total sum of squares.

Consider the 16 scores on the abbreviated XYZ Inventory. The sum of squares will be larger if we take the deviations of each individual from the *grand mean* than if we take the deviations of all 16 participants from their *individual group means*. Taking deviations from the grand mean and squaring them yields the total sum of squares. Taking the deviations from the individual group means yields the *within-groups SS*.

It can be shown mathematically that the total sum of squares is equal to the sum of squares within groups plus the sum of squares between groups.

$$\text{or } SS_T = SS_W + SS_B$$

The SS_T uses squared deviations from the grand mean for all participants. The SS_W uses squared deviations from individual group means for all participants, while the SS_B uses squared deviations of each group mean from the grand mean multiplied by N for the group.

To illustrate the relationship, let's calculate the total SS so we can compare it with the within- and between-groups SS we found. To find the SS_T we first take the deviations of each of our participants from the grand mean, 3.5. We get the following *deviations from the grand mean*:

0.5	3.5	0.5	1.5
1.5	1.5	0.5	0.5
1.5	0.5	0.5	0.5
2.5	0.5	1.5	0.5

Squaring these, we get the following squared deviations from the grand mean:

0.25	12.25	0.25	2.25	
2.25	2.25	0.25	0.25	
2.25	0.25	0.25	0.25	
6.25	0.25	2.25	0.25	
11.00	15.00	3.00	3.00	SST = 11 + 15 + 3 + 3 = 32

Adding the sums along the bottom row, we get our Total Sum of Squares (SS_T), which is 32. Our total sum of squares (32) is equal to the sum of squares within groups (12) plus the sum of squares between groups (20).

$$SS_T = SS_W + SS_B$$
$$32 = 12 + 20$$

Two-Way Analysis of Variance

The ANOVA presented above is known as *one-way analysis of variance* because we are assessing the effects of just one independent variable (dominant function) on the measure of the dependent variable we are using (the XYZ inventory). We classified our participants in just one-way, according to their dominant function. Suppose however we wanted to assess the effects of two variables—for example, both dominant function and level of type development. Then *two-way analysis of variance* can be used.

To illustrate, let's imagine another study. Let's compare the original dominant S, N, T, and F means of college sophomores from page 174 with the XYZ scores of groups of middle-aged college graduates—presumed to have better type development than sophomores—who are dominant Ss, Ns, Ts, and Fs.

Hypotheses. In this experiment the null hypothesis is that there will not be differences in XYZ scores between people with different dominant functions nor between people at different life stages. The alternative or research hypotheses are that there will be differences both related to dominant function and to life stages.

Level of significance. We will set our minimally-acceptable level of significance or alpha at .05.

Collecting data. There are a total of eight groups, one for each combination of dominant function and stage in life. Each group in our experiment has ten participants. The following are mean scores on the XYZ Inventory found for our college sophomores and middle-aged graduates, with row and column means at right and bottom.

	Dominant Functions				
	S	N	T	F	Row $\overline{X}$
Sophomores	47.54	66.06	53.14	57.98	56.18
Graduates	64.97	59.73	58.39	62.27	61.34
Column $\overline{X}$	56.26	62.90	55.77	60.13	

Grand Mean 58.76

Finding the variances. We're not going to go through all the calculations on this one. We only want to see the principles involved. If we were to do the calculations, we would find each person's deviations from three different means–

  • from the mean of his or her individual group mean (for SS_W),

  • from the column mean by dominant function (part of SS_B), and

  • from the row mean by stage in life (part of SS_B).

We would also take deviations between group means and the grand mean for SS_B.

Sums of squares are found in essentially the same way as in one-way ANOVA. We use the following steps to calculate sum of squares:

- *Between groups SS*. Take the deviation of each of our eight group means from the grand mean, square the deviation, multiply the result by the N in the group, then add these squared deviations together.

- *Within groups SS*. Take the deviation of each individual score from the mean of its group, square the deviation, and add these squared deviations across all individuals in all groups.

We will not need to show the calculation of the Total SS (taking each individual deviation from the grand mean), but as before, $SS_T = SS_W + SS_B$.

What is different in two-way ANOVA is that the variance between groups is more complex than in one-way ANOVA. The between-groups variance is an all causes variance, and can be further analyzed into components of variance. To use our example, the between-groups variance will contain

- a component related to the effect of different dominant functions,

- a component related to the effect of stage in life, and

- another component related to the interaction between dominant function and stage in life.

As we look at our means, the effects of maturity seem to be more pronounced for some dominant groups than for others. While most graduates have higher XYZ scores, maturity seems to have a greater enhancing effect for Ss and a negative effect for Ns. The results suggest an interaction between our main variables, dominant function and stage in life.

It can be shown mathematically that the between-groups SS is equal to the SS related to the first variable, plus the SS related to the second variable, plus the SS related to the interaction. Thus, the SS between groups in our experiment will be equal to the SS related to dominant function, plus the SS related to stage in life, plus the SS related to the interaction between dominant function and stage.

$$SS_B = SS_{\text{variable 1}} + SS_{\text{variable 2}} + SS_{\text{variable 1 x variable 2}}$$

To separate out the component parts of the between-groups sum of squares, we follow three steps.

- We separate out the SS related to dominant function (variable 1) by summing the squared deviations of all individuals from their respective dominant (column) mean.

- We separate out the SS related to stage in life (variable 2) by summing the squared deviations of all individuals from their respective stage in life (row) mean.

- We find the SS related to the interaction by a process of elimination. We subtract the variable 1-related SS and the variable 2-related SS from the SS between groups, and the remainder is the interaction-related SS.

$$SS_{variable\ 1\ x\ variable\ 2} = SS_B - (SS_{variable\ 1} + SS_{variable\ 2})$$

Degrees of freedom. We find the variance by dividing each SS by its appropriate d.f. The logic for determining d.f. is the same as in one-way ANOVA. In our experiment, the d.f. for within groups variance is total N - K, or 80 - 8 = 72. The between-groups d.f. is K - 1, or 8 - 1 = 7. The between-groups d.f. of 7 is subdivided further, with 4 - 1 = 3 related to dominant function; 2 - 1 = 1 related to stage in life, and the remaining 3 related to the interaction.

Finding the F-ratio. The F-ratios for possible significance are performed by dividing individually each of the variances related to dominant function, stage, and interaction by the within-groups variance. Any one of these three variance ratios, or combinations of them, may be significant.

If we have three (or more) variables of interest, it is possible to do three-way (or more-way) analysis of variance. The general principles remain the same, though the calculations and interpretation become increasingly complicated.

Chi-Square

The statistical tests we have considered thus far all require *interval* data that is *normally distributed*, that is, scores fall in a more-or-less normal curve. However, if we have *nominal* data, such as frequency counts, then the chi-square (χ^2) test is appropriate when we want to see if we have statistical significance. Chi-square is used frequently in MBTI research because the data often consists of counts of the number of cases of different types observed.

Let's suppose we're attending an Association for Psychological Type (APT) conference and enjoy stopping for an ice cream cone each afternoon at the dairy store located near the conference center. Many of our fellow conference attendees stop by as well, and we note with interest that Extraverts seem to disproportionately choose chocolate ice cream, while Introverts tend toward vanilla and strawberry. This isn't a 31-flavors store!

Hypotheses. In this experiment, the null hypothesis is that there is no difference between Extraverts and Introverts in their choices of ice cream flavors. The alternative or research hypothesis is that there are differences between E–I preferences and flavor choice.

Level of significance. We will use a *two-tailed* test because we have no theoretical basis for assuming a particular preference pattern, and we will be interested in the results whichever direction they come out. We set our minimum level of significance at the .05 level.

Collecting data. We are ready to systematically collect data. The next afternoon we go to the ice cream store again. From name-tags we note the personality type of the person and then we observe their flavor choice. We collect a sample of 20 observations, 10 Extraverts and 10 Introverts, with the following frequencies:

FLAVOR	Vanilla	Chocolate	Strawberry	Row Total
Extraverts	2	7	1	10
Introverts	4	3	3	10
Column Total	6	10	4	20

Each cell in the table has the frequency of conference attendees making each flavor choice, divided by Extraverts and Introverts. Row and column totals, also called marginals, are given for a step we will take in a moment.

Finding Chi-Square. The chi-square test compares frequencies that are actually observed or obtained in our study, called *obtained frequencies*, with the frequencies we would expect, *expected frequencies*, if there really is no relationship between E–I preference and flavor choice, that is, if the null hypothesis is true.

So how do we find our expected frequencies? Let's consider first the 6 of our 20 participants who chose vanilla. If there is no relationship between type and flavor choice and all the differences we saw were due to chance, then there should be no difference in frequency of choosing vanilla for Extraverts and Introverts. Since 6 chose vanilla and we had equal numbers of Es and Is in our sample, we would expect 3 Es and 3 Is to choose vanilla.

To calculate the expected frequency for a cell in our table we multiply the row total for that cell by the column total and divide by the grand total frequency.

For example, the expected frequency for the cell of Es choosing vanilla would be the respective row total (10) multiplied by the respective column total (6), divided by the grand total (20); thus we have

$$10 \times 6 \div 20 = 60 \div 20 = 3$$

as the expected frequency of the cell. Using this procedure, we find the remaining expected frequencies in our table, and put them in parentheses next to the number we actually obtained:

Obtained and (Expected) Frequencies

	Vanilla	Chocolate	Strawberry
Extraverts	2 (3)	7 (5)	1 (2)
Introverts	4 (3)	3 (5)	3 (2)

We find chi-square by subtracting each expected frequency (f_e) from each obtained frequency (f_o), squaring the difference, dividing by the expected frequency, and summing over both rows and columns, or

$$\chi^2 = \Sigma \, \frac{(f_o - f_e)^2}{f_e}$$

For our experiment, we find the following chi-square:

$$\chi^2 = \frac{(2-3)^2}{3} + \frac{(7-5)^2}{5} + \frac{(1-2)^2}{2} + \frac{(4-3)^2}{3} + \frac{(3-5)^2}{5} + \frac{(3-2)^2}{2}$$

$$\chi^2 = \frac{(-1)^2}{3} + \frac{(2)^2}{5} + \frac{(-1)^2}{2} + \frac{(1)^2}{3} + \frac{(-2)^2}{5} + \frac{(1)^2}{2}$$

$$\chi^2 = \frac{1}{3} + \frac{4}{5} + \frac{1}{2} + \frac{1}{3} + \frac{4}{5} + \frac{1}{2}$$

$$\chi^2 = .33 + .80 + .50 + .33 + .80 + .50 = 3.26$$

Degrees of Freedom. The degrees of freedom for a chi-square are the number of rows minus 1 times the number of columns minus 1, or (R - 1)(C - 1). For our experiment, we will have

$$(2 - 1)(3 - 1) = (1)(2) = 2 \text{ d.f.}$$

Finding the Critical Value. To see whether our chi-square of 3.26 is significant, we turn to a chi-square table in a statistics book. We will find that for 2 d.f.

and alpha = .05 (or the .05 level of significance), the critical value is 5.991. Our obtained chi-square of 3.26 is not that high, so we do not have significance. For now we cannot conclude that Extraverts and Introverts differ in ice cream flavor choice.

To determine chi-square, we followed these steps.

- We stated our hypotheses, chose our statistical test (chi-square), set a minimum significance level at .05, and determined our d.f. to be (R-1) multiplied by (C-1).

- We calculated the expected frequency for each cell of the table.

- We subtracted each expected frequency (f_e) from each obtained frequency (f_o).

- We squared the difference between each f_e and f_o.

- We divided each squared difference by f_e.

- We summed the results over all rows.

- We looked in a chi-square table to find the critical value for our degrees of freedom.

Because the result we found (3.26) was less than the critical value for χ^2 (5.991), we concluded that we do not have significance.

You may wonder whether the sample size in our experiment was just too small for a significant relationship to be revealed, and if so, you'd be right. We kept the numbers small here for ease in seeing the calculation of chi-square. Indeed, a rule of thumb is that all expected frequencies should be at least 5 when we set up an experiment for which we'll use chi-square. Quick figuring of what would happen if the same pattern of results were obtained but with twice as many participants reveals a chi-square of 6.53, which would be significant.

Learning Key

t-test: Common inferential statistic, used to test the significance of the difference between 2 means; also used to test whether a correlation coefficient is significant.

Analysis of variance (ANOVA): Technique used for testing the significance of differences between 3 or more means. With two-way (or more-way) ANOVA, we are able to separate out what part of the variance is attributable to each variable, the interaction between the variables, and error.

Chi-square: Commonly used statistical test when data are frequencies. We compare observed frequencies with theoretically expected frequencies to see if what we observed could have happened just by chance.

Does that mean we can go out tomorrow and observe 20 more ice-cream shoppers, and add the results to what we got today? Generally not. Most statistical tests are based on *independent observations*. To make more than one observation on the same individual—unless the statistical test is designed to handle repeated observations—may increase our likelihood of a Type I error, thinking we have significance when really it was a chance result. Because we would have no way to assure that we wouldn't be observing some of the same people buying ice cream tomorrow as we did today, we'll need an independent sample tomorrow and not reuse any of today's data.

Appendix C describes the Selection Ratio Type Table, an application of chi-square for type research.

Exercises and Questions to Check Your Understanding

1. **Place in the blank the letter of the significance test that would be used with each experiment described below. A significance test may be used more than once.**

   a. *t test*

   b. *one-way Analysis of Variance*

   c. *two-way Analysis of Variance*

   d. *chi-Square*

   e. Spearman-Brown Prophesy Correction

   _____A. 100 blindfolded people are asked to choose which of 3 colas they prefer. We find 37 people prefer Cola A, 49 people prefer Cola B, and 14 people prefer Cola C. Is this likely a chance finding?

   _____B. 25 men and 25 women complete the XYZ Inventory. Based on the means and SDs we obtained, do men receive significantly larger scores?

   _____C. A group of nursing home patients with dementia are randomly assigned to one of three treatment conditions. After a month, a standard memory and orientation test is administered, from which we get means and SDs for each group.

   _____D. We correlate XYZ scores and age in a group of 200 people. Is the correlation coefficient we got likely a chance finding?

_____ E. Students in an elementary school are exposed to one of two different teaching styles for learning math. They are given a standard math test at the beginning and end of the term, so we get a change score that reflects the amount of learning that occurred. We get means and SDs for each teaching style for each of the 4 grade levels.

2. For each of the following results, what decision should be made about the null hypothesis at the .05 level? Circle the correct decision. Remember that < means *less than* and > means *greater than*.

A. $\chi^2 = 4.11$, d.f. $= 1$, $p < .05$ Accept H_o Reject H_o

B. $\chi^2 = 2.82$, d.f. $= 2$, $p > .05$ Accept H_o Reject H_o

APPENDIX C

The Selection Ratio Type Table

Sometimes an assessment instrument has particular properties that require a statistical technique that is specific for that instrument. An example is the **Selection Ratio Type Table (SRTT)** used with the MBTI assessment and other type instruments. The SRTT is based on the chi-square test of significance which is illustrated in Appendix B.

If you are using this book in MBTI certification training, this section about SRTT is required reading. If you are using the book in another course, your instructor may determine that this is an optional section.

Overview

The SRTT is a special statistical procedure to compare the distribution of type in one group with that in another group by comparing the type tables of the two groups. A type table is the frequency distribution layout of the sixteen types. Each comparison in the table—comparing a type with the same type in the other group—is called a **Self-Selection Ratio (SSR)** or **Selection Ratio (SR)**. This ratio is also called the **Index of Attraction**. Each of these three terms means the same thing. If the Index of Attraction is greater than 1.00, there are more people of that type in the sample group than we would expect to find. People of that type are over-represented. If the Index of Attraction is under 1.00, people of that type are under-represented.

The Selection Ratio Type Table comes from a computer program originally developed for Isabel Myers during her longitudinal medical student studies. Myers collected type data on a large group of medical students and then conducted a follow-up study years later to see what medical specialties they chose. For each type she analyzed the specialties significantly chosen or avoided and named the statistic she used the **selection ratio** or **self-selection ratio**, because she was studying the students' selection of their medical specialties. The selection ratio was simply a ratio that compared the number of the type choosing a specialty with the number that would be expected to choose that specialty, based on the proportion of that type in the total sample of physicians.

An alternate term, **Index of Attraction**, comes from the same source. Myers was interested in whether certain personality types were attracted to particular medical specialties.

When an SRTT is used, the type table displayed is called the *sample* or *group* tabulated. The type table to which it is compared is called the *base population*. If our sample is part of the base population, the SRTT will state that the sample and base are *dependent*. If the sample and base are from two different populations, the SRTT report states that the sample and base are *independent*.

To illustrate how the SRTT works, look at the SRTT in table C.1, page 194. The sample is a group of 75 persons elected to Phi Beta Kappa in the 1982 Follow Up to a 1972 University of Florida Counseling Study done by the Center for Applications of Psychological Type.

The note near the bottom of table C.1 states that the base population is a group of 1,878 1972 freshmen who eventually graduated, and that the sample and base are dependent. In other words, the 75 in the sample were part of the 1,878. Had the base population been a group of which these 75 were not a part, such as a large sample of students at other universities, the sample would have been independent. Dependent samples are quite common in SRTT studies and are

---

Learning Key

Selection Ratio Type Table (SRTT): Technique to compare the distribution of type in a sample with the distribution of type in a base, or reference, population.

Self-Selection Ratio (SSR) or Selection Ratio (SR): Ratio of the percentage of a type in a sample with the percentage of that same type in a base population. An SSR or SR below 1.00 indicates under-selection—fewer of that type or preference occurred in the sample than would have been expected—and an SSR or SR over 1.00 indicates over-selection.

Index of Attraction: another term for SSR or SR; I = SSR = SR

considered somewhat easier to interpret. Table C.2, page 195, shows the type table for the 1,878 freshmen used as the base population.

Each cell of the type table part of the SRTT includes

- the number (N) of people in the sample with that type,
- the percentage (%) of that type in the sample, and
- the Index of Attraction (I).

Looking at the ISTJ cell, we see that 6 of the 75 freshmen elected to Phi Beta Kappa (8% of the group) were ISTJs. The Index of Attraction is 1.12. This is a ratio and is calculated by dividing the percentage in the sample by the comparable percentage in the base. In this case the percentage of ISTJs in the Phi Beta Kappa sample, 8.00%, is divided by the percentage of ISTJs in the base population of 1878 freshmen, 7.14%.

$$I = \% \text{ in sample} \div \% \text{ in base}$$
$$I = 8.00 \div 7.14 = 1.12.$$

The I of 1.12 suggests that ISTJs were slightly more likely to be elected to Phi Beta Kappa than would be expected from their percentage in the base population. Another way to state this is to say that ISTJs were slightly *overrepresented* or *overselected* among those elected to Phi Beta Kappa.

INFJs were also overrepresented in this sample. For INFJs, I = 2.20. This tells us that 2.2 times as many INFJs were found in this sample as would have been expected from the base population. We see that 2.2 times as many INFJs were elected to Phi Beta Kappa than would be expected if type were not a factor.

To see whether an Index of Attraction is significant, we look for a symbol next to the value of the I. Footnotes tell us that * indicates significance at the .05 level, ** indicates the .01 level, and *** indicates the .001 level. The finding of I = 1.12 for ISTJs is not significant. We can see that the Index of Attraction for INFJs is significant at the .05 level, and the I for INTJ is significant at the .001 level. Because I was greater than 1.00 in each of these cases, we know that there are more people in that cell of the table than we would expect from the numbers in the base population. Each of these types is overrepresented or overselected.

If the Index of Attraction is less than 1.00, there are fewer in that cell than expected. People of that type are *underrepresented*. The Index of Attraction for ESFJs of 0.15 is significant at the .05 level. There are several Is that are below 1.00, but only this one is significant.

The SRTT may compare ratios only for the 16 types, or it may include frequencies and percentages of each of the 8 preferences as well as 20 two-letter combinations, as we have in table C.1, giving us a total of 44 comparisons.

Note the significant findings on three of the MBTI dichotomies: Is, Ns and Ts are significantly overrepresented—and Es, Ss and Fs are significantly under-represented—among those elected to Phi Beta Kappa. While there are no significant differences on J–P, J is significantly related in combination with I and N (above expectation) and S (below expectation).

A word of caution: If we are doing tests of significance and choose the .05 level of significance, probability tells us 5 of every 100 significance tests we calculate are apt to be significant by chance alone. With 44 comparisons, we can anticipate a couple of comparisons will be significant at the .05 level just by chance each time we do an SRTT. This is the problem of Type I errors we met in chapter 3. We noted that 5 of every 100 significance tests we calculate are likely to be significant *by chance alone* if we are using a .05 level of significance.

If you look at our SRTT example, it is obvious that much more than chance significance occurred. Table C.1 had 6 differences significant at .05, 3 at .01 (only 1 in 100 of these likely would be due to chance), and 8 at .001 (1 in 1000 by chance). We can be fairly confident we have more than chance here. However, we cannot be certain any particular finding is not a chance one. Probability never allows us to be totally certain.

Because of the possibility of by-chance-alone significance, one principle is to use a conservative approach in interpreting SRTTs. When we have specific hypotheses, we can plan ahead of time to consider only certain ones of the 44 chi-squares that relate to our hypotheses. We will look at the others, but only as information to consider in planning further research.

Another principle is to not report significant findings within the two-preference combinations when the effect has already been shown in the results for the single preferences. Looking again at table C.1, we see that both Extraversion and Sensing are under-selected among the Phi Beta Kappa electees. It is not surprising, then, that the combination ES is also significantly underselected. We can disregard this last finding in our interpretation because we don't need to use combination findings that only repeat what we already know.

It is also judicious to use caution in reporting findings for a group unless the ratios for all types within the group show the same direction. For example, to report a finding for ES types, we will want to look at ratios for all four types in the group (ESTP, ESFP, ESTJ, ESFJ) to see that all four ratios are in the same direction.

The SRTT is an important part of MBTI research, and frequently appears in research articles about type. The SRTT program is available from the Center for Applications of Psychological Type for use on personal computers.

Exercises and Questions to Check Your Understanding

Look at Tables C.1 and C.2, pages 194–195. Answer the following questions for ENTJ and ISFJ.

 A. How many Phi Beta Kappa (PBK) graduates in this study had this type?

 B. What percent of the base population had this type?

 C. What percent of the PBK grads had this type?

 D. What is the Index of Attraction (I) for the PBK grads?

 E. How does the frequency among PBK grads of this type compare with the base population?

	ENTJ	ISFJ
A.	_____	_____
B.	_____	_____
C.	_____	_____
D.	_____	_____
E.	_____	_____

Table C.1

Phi Beta Kappas

N = 75

	SENSING		INTUITION	
	THINKING	FEELING	FEELING	THINKING

ISTJ	ISFJ	INFJ	INTJ
N = 6	N = 3	N = 8	N = 10
% = 8.00	% = 4.00	% = 10.67	% = 13.33
I = 1.12	I = 0.48	I = 2.20*	I = 3.43***
■■■■■■■■	■■■■	■■■■■■■■■■	■■■■■■■■■■ ■■■
ISTP	**ISFP**	**INFP**	**INTP**
N = 2	N = 2	N = 10	N = 8
% = 2.67	% = 2.67	% = 13.33	% = 10.67
I = 1.04	I = 0.51	I = 1.20	I = 2.30*
■■	■■	■■■■■■■■■■ ■■■	■■■■■■■■■■
ESTP	**ESFP**	**ENFP**	**ENTP**
N = 1	N = 2	N = 8	N = 2
% = 1.33	% = 2.67	% = 10.67	% = 2.67
I = 0.56	I = 0.53	I = 0.73	I = 0.61
■	■■	■■■■■■■■■■	■■
ESTJ	**ESFJ**	**ENFJ**	**ENTJ**
N = 1	N = 1	N = 5	N = 6
% = 1.33	% = 1.33	% = 6.67	% = 8.00
I = 0.19	I = 0.15	I = 1.10	I = 2.09
■	■	■■■■■■	■■■■■■■■

Vertical labels (right side of grid, top to bottom): JUDGMENT — INTROVERSION PERCEPTION — PERCEPTION EXTRAVERSION JUDGMENT

	N	%	I
E	26	34.67	0.66**
I	49	65.33	1.37**
S	18	24.00	0.52***
N	57	76.00	1.42***
T	36	48.00	1.33*
F	39	52.00	0.81*
J	40	53.33	1.07
P	35	46.67	0.93
I J	27	36.00	1.49*
I P	22	29.33	1.25
EP	13	17.33	0.65
EJ	13	17.33	0.67
ST	10	13.33	0.69
SF	8	10.67	0.39**
NF	31	41.33	1.13
NT	26	34.67	2.07***
SJ	11	14.67	0.47**
SP	7	9.33	0.61
NP	28	37.33	1.07
NJ	29	38.67	2.07***
TJ	23	30.67	1.39
TP	13	17.33	1.24
FP	22	29.33	0.81
FJ	17	22.67	0.81
I N	36	48.00	1.96***
EN	21	28.00	0.97
I S	13	17.33	0.75
ES	5	6.67	0.29
ET	10	13.33	0.75
EF	16	21.33	0.62*
I F	23	30.67	1.04
I T	26	34.67	1.90***
Sdom	12	16.00	0.70
Ndom	28	37.33	1.35
Tdom	17	22.67	1.24
Fdom	18	24.00	0.77

Note: ■ = One Percent; Base Population = 1972 Freshmen who graduated from University of Florida, N=1878. Sample and base are dependent. Subjects were graduates nominated to the Phi Beta Kappa honor society (56% female, 44% male).

Source: Macdaid, McCaulley & Kainz, 1982. The University of Florida Freshmen Study: Ten Year Follow-Up.

I = self selection index
* = p > .05
** = p > .01
*** = p > .001

Table C.2

	SENSING		INTUITION	
	THINKING	FEELING	FEELING	THINKING
	ISTJ	**ISFJ**	**INFJ**	**INTJ**
	N = 134	N = 156	N = 91	N = 73
	% = 7.14	% = 8.31	% = 4.85	% = 3.89
	■■■■■■■	■■■■■■■■	■■■■■	■■■■
	ISTP	**ISFP**	**INFP**	**INTP**
	N = 48	N = 98	N = 209	N = 87
	% = 2.56	% = 5.22	% = 11.13	% = 4.63
	■■■	■■■■■	■■■■■■■■■■ ■	■■■■■
	ESTP	**ESFP**	**ENFP**	**ENTP**
	N = 45	N = 95	N = 275	N = 82
	% = 2.40	% = 5.06	% = 14.64	% = 4.37
	■■	■■■■■	■■■■■■■■■■ ■■■■	■■■■
	ESTJ	**ESFJ**	**ENFJ**	**ENTJ**
	N = 135	N = 164	N = 114	N = 72
	% = 7.19	% = 8.73	% = 6.07	% = 3.83
	■■■■■■■	■■■■■■■■	■■■■■■	■■■■

Left side vertical labels: JUDGMENT / INTROVERSION / PERCEPTION (top half); PERCEPTION / EXTRAVERSION / JUDGMENT (bottom half)

■ = 1% of sample

Type	N	%
E	982	52.29
I	896	47.71
S	875	46.59
N	1003	53.41
T	676	36.00
F	1202	64.00
J	939	50.00
P	939	50.00
IJ	454	24.17
IP	442	23.54
EP	497	26.46
EJ	485	25.83
ST	362	19.28
SF	513	27.32
NF	689	36.69
NT	350	16.72
SJ	589	31.36
SP	286	15.23
NP	653	34.77
NJ	314	18.64
TJ	414	22.04
TP	262	13.95
FP	677	36.05
FJ	525	27.96
IN	460	24.49
EN	543	28.91
IS	436	23.22
ES	439	23.38
ET	334	17.78
EF	648	34.50
IF	554	29.50
IT	342	18.21
S dom	430	22.90
N dom	521	27.74
T dom	342	18.21
F dom	585	31.15

Data collected by Gerald Macdaid, Mary McCaulley, and Richard Kainz of CAPT during 1972, and followed up in 1982, using Form F. Subjects were a subset of over 2500 students who had been entering students at the University of Florida in 1972. Subjects were all students who graduated. The sample was comprised of 57% males and 43% females.

APPENDIX

One-Tailed and Two-Tailed Tests

As noted in chapter 3, a research hypothesis in an experiment can be either directional or nondirectional. To use our example of comparing Extraverts and Introverts with the XYZ Inventory, we can just hypothesize that there will be a difference between Es and Is on the test (nondirectional), or we can hypothesize that one or the other will have the higher scores (directional). If our hypothesis is nondirectional, we will use a **two-tailed** statistical test. If the hypothesis is directional, for example, that Es will have higher scores, then we can use a **one-tailed** test.

To understand what all this tail business means, look at the distributions in figure D.1. The tails are the upper and lower ends of the distribution, where the curve comes almost to a point with the baseline.

In a test of significance, we are trying to determine how likely it is that the results we obtain in an experiment or set of observations could have occurred merely by chance. If we did our experiment lots of times and there really were no differences between Es and Is on XYZ scores other than chance factors, we'd expect to get somewhat different results each time due to sampling error; sometimes Es would get higher scores, sometimes they'd get lower scores, but the differences would average out to 0. If we were to plot the difference between XYZ scores for Es and XYZ scores for Is across all these experiments, assuming no real differences between Es and Is, the results would look something like the normal distributions in figure D.1 (page 198), where the dashed vertical line in the middle represents the null hypothesis of no difference. If there really is nothing but chance going on

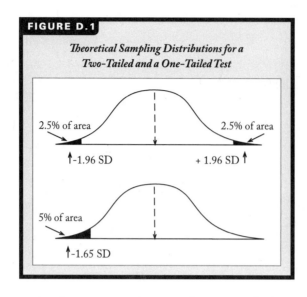

FIGURE D.1

Theoretical Sampling Distributions for a Two-Tailed and a One-Tailed Test

2.5% of area   2.5% of area

↑ -1.96 SD   + 1.96 SD ↑

5% of area

↑ -1.65 SD

in our results, we'd expect differences to cluster near the middle (difference of 0) with fewer and fewer cases as we get away from the middle and into the tails of the distribution.

But suppose there really is something other than chance going on. Our results are apt to be away from the middle, in one of the tails, where either Es or Is would be getting larger scores. As part of our research design, we designate a part of the area under the curve, in the tails, as the **critical area** or **rejection area**. If the value we calculate in our significance test falls in this area of the statistical distribution we are using, we will say our research results are significant, and we will be able to reject the null hypothesis.

If we use a .05 significance level, we will designate 5% of the area under the curve in the statistic's distribution as the **critical area**. If you look back at figure 2.7 on page 23, you will note that 2.2% of a normal distribution is above +2 SD and 2.2% is below -2 SD. In a normal distribution, 2.5% is beyond 1.96 SD, so the area below -1.96 and above +1.96 SD makes up 5% of the distribution. This would be our critical area if we were using a two-tailed test.

We would use a two-tailed test if we were concerned about *either* a high or low result, for example, Es outperforming Is, or Is outperforming Es. We might have a hunch that the results would turn out a particular way, but suppose we were wrong. We'd want to be able to detect a significant result even if the results came out differently than we expected. This is what is portrayed in the top distribution in figure D.1. If the actual difference found is greater than 1.96 SD above or below the mean, it will fall in the shaded area of the distribution. We will be able to reject the null hypothesis, and our experimental results will be *significant*.

Suppose, however, that we were only concerned with a result in one direction. Then we could put all of our 5% in one tail and would need a result beyond only 1.65 SD to have significance. Then the bottom distribution in figure D.1, or its mirror image with the critical area in the upper tail, would represent our statistical decision area. In this case a smaller difference between groups would turn out to be significant, because the result would only need to fall at least 1.65 SDs from the mean. If a two-tailed test were used, the result would need to be at least 1.96 SDs from the mean. Thus we would have a better chance of rejecting the null hypothesis and finding significance with a one-tailed test.

To illustrate, suppose we discover that one discount store brand of light bulb is a lot cheaper than the national brand we've been using, and the manufacturer claims these cheaper bulbs will last as long as the expensive ones. To test whether this cheaper brand of bulbs is as good as our regular brand, we set up groups of cheaper and regular bulbs to see how long they last. In planning the statistics for this little experiment, we can use a one-tailed test because our only concern is that the cheaper bulbs last as long as our regular ones. If these cheaper bulbs last longer than our regular bulbs, that's just a nice bonus.

In actual practice, two-tailed tests are used most of the time, even when we are quite sure the results will be in one particular direction. Even if we are pretty confident that Extraverts will get higher scores on the XYZ Inventory, it's always possible we guessed wrong, or that the people we observed weren't a representative sample, and Introverts in our experimental sample will get the higher scores. We'd want to know if this finding was just a fluke, or if we could have some confidence that our result reflected something about the E–I difference or the nature of the XYZ Inventory we hadn't known before. It is tempting to use one-tailed tests so we have a better chance of getting significance, but we typically are well advised to use a two-tailed test.

When you are reading a journal article where a one-tailed test is used, it is a good idea to ask yourself whether the author really was justified in using it. What one worries about is the possibility that a two-tailed test was originally used, but it did not yield significance, so the author decided to use a one-tailed test instead. Doing that increases the likelihood of a Type I error (refer to page 61 for information about errors). Note, however, that some significance tests, such as ANOVA, always use a one-tailed test of significance.

Learning Key

One-tailed and two-tailed tests: The rejection area for a test of significance can be placed in one tail of the distribution, or divided between the two tails. A one-tailed test is used with a directional hypothesis when only one direction is important. If a difference either way could be important, a two-tailed test is used.

Critical area or rejection area: Area in one or both tails of a statistical distribution where, if the results of a significance test fall there, we will be able to reject the null hypothesis and say our results are significant.

APPENDIX E

Chapter 2   Descriptive Statistics

1. A & D are frequency distributions, telling us numerically in A how many got each score and graphically in D. B is a correlation scatter plot, and C is just a listing of ranks.

2. A. d. Ratio. 0 miles is really zero, nothing.

    B. b. Ordinal

    C. a. Nominal

    D. c. Interval only. A score of 0 on an achievement test is not a true zero, but is arbitrary. It may be the lowest possible score on the test, but it does not indicate absolutely no knowledge.

3. A. 5

    B. 4

    C. 4

    D. 2-9 (or 7)

4. A. +1.5   -2   +0.25

    B.   93   4   60

    C. 48 to 72

5. A. (1) number in the sample

        (2) mean of the sample

        (3) standard deviation

B.	-3SD	-2SD	-1SD	$\overline{X}$	+1SD	+2SD	+3SD
Mechanical	65	80	95	110	125	140	155
Musical	30	38	46	54	62	70	78

C. (1) -0.5 approximately

(2) +1.0

D. Use Figure 2.8 to check your answer

E. Musical

F. Between 80 and 140. Approximately 2 SD ($2 \times 15 = 30$) − and + the mean.

6. A. Group Y

B. 0.0   If everyone has the same score, there is no variability.

7. A. -.63

B. +.53

C. -.72

8. A. +

B. +

C. −

9. A. Perfect positive correlation

B. Perfect negative correlation

C. No correlation

D. Moderate positive correlation

E. Moderately high negative correlation

10. A. Correlation coefficient (Pearson Product-Moment correlation coefficient)

B. R-squared. Variance accounted for. Converts correlation to a percentage.

11. Square a correlation to get a percentage

12. A. .16 or 16%

B. .25 or 25%

C. .56 or 56%

Chapter 3   Inferential Statistics

1. A. b.

B. a.

C. d.

2. C

3. A. .01 is "higher" than .05

4. ** says "significant at the .01 level"—or the probability is less than 1 in 100 that this was just a chance result

5. A. No
    B. p >.05 tells us the difference was not significant, or the probability was greater than 5 in 100 that this result was just a chance finding

6. A. Yes
    B. "Null hypothesis was rejected" and "p < .01" each indicate significance

7. B and C. A and D both deal with public safety and require much higher levels of significance, perhaps .0001 or higher.

8. A. The larger the sample, the less likely any difference will be a chance one, so we are more apt to find significance and thus be able to reject the null hypothesis.

9. A. T
    B. T
    C. F   Using a lower level of significance would increase Type I errors.
    D. F   Rejecting a true null hypothesis is a Type I error.
    E. F   There is no simple way to know what our risk of a Type II error is.
    F. F   We may be able to reduce them, but not eliminate them.
    G. T

Chapter 4   Reliability

1. D   A, B, and C all can have an impact on reliability

2. C

3. A. a, c   Might even have alternate forms, so could be b as well
    B. c
    C. a   Could use c also
    D. a   Could use c also
    E. a, b
    F. c

4. A. Test-retest
        Don't make this too complicated; look at headers and footers!
    B. Reliability is higher for older groups.
    C. Reliability appears higher for groups with more education.
    D. For university sophomores, at least, reliability is somewhat lower when the period between test and retest is longer

E.   .36 or 36% for the correlation of .60

5.   C.   The SE_{meas} helps us know how much error there is, but not where it comes from.

6.   Between 99 and 107 (approximately). Confidence limits at the 95% level are 1.96 times the SE_{meas} above and below the obtained score. We multiply 1.96 x 2.10 (roughly 2 x 2 = 4) to get the amount we add and subtract from the obtained score of 103. If you don't want an approximation, 1.96 x 2.10 is 4.12, so the confidence limits would be 98.88 and 107.12.

7.   C   A   B   D

Chapter 5   Validity

1.   B, D, and E are all correct

2.   Correlation coefficient

3.   We must square the correlation coefficients so we know what percentage of variance is accounted for.

4.   A. b

     B. c

     C. a

     D. e

5.   A.   The significant correlations link Extraversion with Autonomy, Self-Confidence, and Sociability (negative correlations) and link Introversion with Deference and Self-Sufficiency (positive correlations). The correlations are all consistent with the usual meaning of Extraversion-Introversion, so they constitute convergent validity evidence.

     B.   Intelligence, masculinity-femininity, religiosity, and suspiciousness are different constructs than Extraversion–Introversion, so the lack of any significant correlation with these scales constitutes discriminant validity evidence.

     C.   No. Correlation tells us of relationships, not that two things are the same or interchangeable.

6.   A   We must have reliability to have validity.

7.   A, B, D, E   The purpose is not to impress clients. Insurance companies may use experts' knowledgeable about reliability and validity to decide what tests they will pay for and they will expect practitioners to be knowledgeable, but they probably won't quiz them about it.

Chapter 6   Norms and Usability

1. A. Yes
   B. No
   C. No
   D. Yes

2. A. base rate
   B. practical usefulness
   C. false positive
   D. cutoff score
   E. false negative, specificity

Appendix B—More Significance Tests Illustrated

1. A. d
   B. a
   C. b
   D. a
   E. c

2. A. Reject H_o; result is significant
   B. Accept H_o; result is not significant

Appendix C—The Selection Ratio Type Table

A.	6	3
B.	3.83	8.31
C.	8.00	4.00
D.	2.09	0.48
E.	higher (overselected)	lower (underselected)

References and Selected Bibliography

Aiken, L. R. 1994. *Psychological testing and assessment, 8th ed.* Boston: Allyn and Bacon.

American Educational Research Association, American Psychological Association, and National Council on Measurement in Education. 1999. *Standards for educational and psychological testing.* Washington, DC: American Educational Research Association.

Anastasi, A. 1988. *Psychological testing, 6th ed.* New York: Macmillan.

Bayne, R. 2005. *Ideas and evidence: Critical reflections on MBTI® theory and practice.* Gainesville, FL: Center for Applications of Psychological Type.

Bradley, M. E. 2003. Journal articles: Primary source. Retrieved 5/6/03 from www.frostburg.edu/psyc/mbradley/journalarticles.html

Cronbach, L. J. 1984. *Essentials of psychological testing, 4nd ed.* New York: Harper and Row.

Garson, G. D. 2006. Latent class analysis. Retrieved from www2.chass.ncsu.edu/garson/pa765/latclass.htm.

Hood, A. B. and R. W. Johnson. 2007. *Assessment in counseling: A guide to the use of psychological assessment procedures, 4th ed.* Alexandria, VA: American Counseling Association.

Kaplan, R. M and D. P. Saccuzzo. 2005. *Psychological testing: Principles, applications, and issues, 6th ed.* Belmont, CA: Wadsworth.

Kimble, G. A. 1978. *How to use (and misuse) statistics.* Englewood Cliffs, NJ: Prentice-Hall.

Lawrence, G. 1993. *People types & tiger stripes, 3rd ed.* Gainesville, FL: Center for Applications of Psychological Type.

Macdaid, G. P. 2003. Research approaches using the MBTI® instrument. In J. A. Provost and S. Anchors, *Using the MBTI® instrument in colleges and universities.* Gainesville, FL: Center for Applications of Psychological Type.

McCaulley, M. H. 1985. The Selection Ratio Type Table: A research strategy for comparing type distributions, *Journal of Psychological Type*, 10, 46–56.

Meltzoff, J. 1998. *Critical thinking about research: Psychology and related fields.* Washington, DC: American Psychological Association.

Mitchell, M. L. and J. M. Jolley. 2004. *Research design explained, 5th ed.* Belmont, CA: Wadsworth.

Morgan, C. T. and R. A. King. 1966. *Introduction to psychology, 3rd ed.* New York: McGraw-Hill.

Munro, B. H., M. A. Visintainer, and E. B. Page. 1986. *Statistical methods for health care research.* Philadelphia: J. B. Lippincott.

Myers, I. B., M. H. McCaulley, N. L. Quenk, and A. L. Hammer. 1998. *Manual: A guide to the development and use of the Myers-Briggs Type Indicator, 3rd ed.* Palo Alto, CA: Consulting Psychologists Press.

Nieswiadomy, R. M. 1998. *Foundations of nursing research, 3rd ed.* Stamford, CT: Appleton & Lange.

Pelham, B. W. and H. Blanton. 2007. *Conducting research in psychology: Measuring the weight of smoke, 3rd ed.* Belmont, CA: Thomson Wadsworth

Shavelson, R. J. 1988. *Statistical reasoning for the behavioral sciences, 2nd ed.* Boston: Allyn and Bacon.

Stanovich, K. E. 2007. *How to think straight about psychology, 8th ed.* Boston: Allyn and Bacon.

Trochim, W. M. K. 2001. *The research methods knowledge base, 2nd ed.* Cincinnati, OH: Atomic Dog Publishing.

Uebersax, J. S. 2001. Latent class analysis frequently asked questions. Retrieved from http://ourworld.compuserve.com/homepages/jsuebersax/faq.htm

Ullman, N. R. 1978. *Elementary statistics: An applied approach.* New York: Wiley.

Index